MW00934123

"Your personal stories and reflecti parts of the book. When you t characteristics that you admired th. was very tender and reassuring. The lessons you learned from Hutch and all the mentors (coaches/students) you had along the way provided you an opportunity to not only share your story but their story as well.

As I read this book, I felt like your primary goal was to make this world a better place by sharing your experiences and the leadership strand was woven throughout the book effectively. I think you should be very proud of what you have accomplished!"

> *Dr. Susan Pecinovsky*
> *President*
> *Iowa Association for Supervision and Curriculum Development (ASCD)*

"*When Life Meets Coaching* gives readers great insight into the highs and lows of coaching and teaching at the high school level. Coach Klaahsen reflects on his coaching journey in great detail and humor. Everyone that reads *When Life Meets Coaching* will take something positive from his book. I highly recommend reading *When Life Meets Coaching*."

> *Jason Eslinger*
> *Assistant Director*
> *Iowa Girls High School Athletic Union (IGHSAU)*

"Excellent Read – Coach Klaahsen captures the essence of the coaching life, embracing obstacles as opportunities along the way. His passion for the journey shines through the high and lows of a coaching journey."

> *Dan Mason*
> *Athletic Director*
> *North Iowa Area Community College*

"Your text is clean and easy to read. As a sports fan, I like the name dropping, of course. I like the way you blend personal stories with the x's and o's."

> *John Naughton*
> *Sports Reporter*
> *Des Moines Register*

When Life Meets Coaching

One Coach's Journey Through the Courts, Fields, and Classrooms of Iowa

Curt Klaahsen

DEDICATION

To my dad, who was a perfect example of love, compassion, work ethic, and strength during rough times that I hope to emulate the rest of my life. I also think of all of the family and friends we have lost over the years who have impacted my life greatly.

ACKNOWLEDGMENTS

A big thanks to everyone who has supported this book-writing journey. Special props to my wife for her work with the layout and design of the book. -A huge thanks to my great friend and colleague, Margie Steinberg for her amazing work as the chief editor of the book and being able to make sense of my scribblings! Also thanks to Tom Kirby, Jody Maske, and my mom for looking through the content and accuracy of the stories. Gratitude to Brett Hollander and Jim Kirby for the use of photos in the book. A final thanks to Ethan Miller, author of *The 6 Keys to Leading with Intention* for his support and great advice on how to get the book published.

I would especially like to acknowledge all of the fellow teachers and coaches I have worked with over the years. Each of you has impacted me in so many ways and your passion and dedication to serving our youth is off the charts. It is tough to be an educator in today's world, and our students and athletes are so fortunate to have such amazing people to learn from every day of their educational experience.

I would like to thank all of my former and current students and athletes who have been willing to be accepting of instruction and who have worked so hard at tasks and activities that many times are very challenging. I have learned a great deal from each of you as well and you are all part of my extended "family." I hope I have been able to positively impact your lives in some small way.

I have been surrounded by great people and role model starting with my parents and going through my siblings, their spouses and kids, uncles, aunts, cousins, and many more-so many memories, so much fun, and so much love! My siblings and I were so blessed with parents who were always there for us, gave us unconditional love, and held us accountable for our actions. Finally, I would like to thank the person in my family who probably has been in my life the least amount of time but has impacted my life as much as anyone - my wife, Margo. For over 16 years, she has supported my passions and let me do what I want while always being behind the scenes and telling me the way it is to keep me grounded and to keep me humble. This journey would not be the same without her!

CONTENTS

PREFACE

The word "coach" has many different meanings to many different people. Most people think of athletics and the coach as the person who leads or instructs a sports team. In recent times, you hear the word "coach" used much more often as we have life coaches for health and well being, instructional coaches in education, and many other areas that people are now utilizing coaches or mentors.

As I look back, coaching has always been a part of my life. I learned to read by looking at sports pages and attended many games early in life where I watched the game and studied what coaches did. I had coaches at school who taught me the fundamentals of the game and kept me motivated to keep playing. Ultimately, once my playing career ended, my love of sports led me to continue to be involved by entering the coaching profession which continues today and has blessed me in so many ways. In 2016, I moved from being a classroom teacher for 28 years to a role as an instructional coach where I currently work with teachers of all subject matters to increase student learning.

As my career in education starts to wind down, I've become more cognizant of how fortunate I have been throughout my life, and it's because of the amazing people that have either been a part of my family, have been friends or acquaintances, or have been people I have worked with in education. I feel I have been incredibly blessed to have jobs that I enjoyed getting ready for and never dreaded what was to come. Although there have been many challenges throughout the years, there have been many opportunities, and it has mostly been through the people I have met and the relationships that have been built.

As I have thought about this, I've realized that every one of these people has "coached" me in some way, and ultimately, everyone we meet becomes a small part of who we are. It doesn't matter if it is one of the five NCAA Division I athletes I have coached, athletes that played a lot, or athletes that never got in the game, I am lucky in that I have learned much more from everyone I have met and worked with than I have ever taught or coached others.

A few years ago, I was talking to a good friend of mine, and I shared a couple of stories from my past of people I have worked with and how they impacted my life. My friend said, "You have had a lot of great experiences and awesome people in your life. You should write a book!" The more I thought about it, the more I realized that I should start writing my ideas down as 1) I don't have children, and this was a way to keep track of everything that has happened in my life, and 2) the lessons I have learned may be helpful to others who haven't had the experiences I have had. Ultimately, when our life ends, our legacy will not be about material possessions or how many titles we've had. It will come down to what kind of person we have been, how have we impacted others, and what we have built that will last well beyond our lives.

The book is written in chronological order and throughout the stories I tell, you will see that I have bolded the lessons I've learned from the people I've met and the experiences I've had throughout my career. You have undoubtedly seen many of these lessons previously, but it's always good to be reminded of them with real-life examples, and hopefully, you will be reminded of the people who have influenced you and the lessons they have taught you!

I apologize in advance for those who I have left out because there isn't enough room to write about everyone I have come into contact with who has influenced me! It has been an amazing journey! I also understand that most of you probably have worked with and learned from as many amazing people as I have! I hope some day you will write about those people who have influenced you in so many ways. I have made an "editorial" choice and I have decided not to name athletes that I mention in the book but will name the adults that are referenced. My hope is that if this book positively impacts even one person in some fashion, then it has been a successful venture. I hope that person is you!

CHAPTER 1

JUST A FARM KID FROM NORTHWEST IOWA

Teachers and Coaches Do Have Lifetime Influence

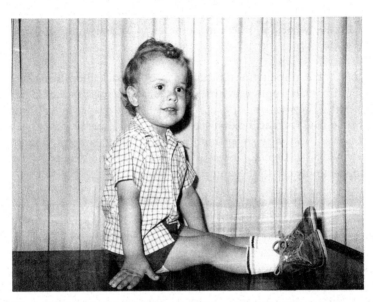

I grew up on a farm close to the small town of George, Iowa, population about a 1000. It was a typical Midwestern small town upbringing with lots of hard work, great people around us, and our entire family close. We didn't have a lot, but had everything we needed. My parents moved to the farm in 1962 (I was born in 1965) so I spent my youth on a farm.

I don't remember a lot about my early childhood, although I have the scar to prove that I had an emergency appendectomy when I was seven months old! Mom says I was a great baby (ha!) and suddenly I started crying hysterically for a long stretch of time. My parents took me to the doctor, and my white blood count was at 15,000 and mounting. The doctor stopped counting and sent me directly to the hospital for surgery! I just had taken a bottle of milk so they had to pump my stomach.

Because of that and the surgery (and having to be held down), for a long time, I had a great fear of anyone dressed in white. My parents have shared that when the Dean Martin Show would come on (he always dressed in white), and he came sliding down a pole, I screamed as loud as I could! I think I've gotten over that for the most part! I may have the record for earliest appendectomy ever, however!

Another "fear" I had was of water. I just hated having something touching my head and again, it went back to my surgery. The folks enrolled me in swimming lessons at age five, and I remember being fine the first day...until they made me put my head under water. Then the panic set in. I barely made it through the day, and that was my last swimming lesson! I can remember people telling me that I'd always regret not being able to swim. I can't say I have, and although I enjoy watching others in the water, I'm fine with not being in the water myself.

I probably did not fit the typical kid profile back then because I hated cartoons and basically only watched sports shows. I was fascinated by sports, and I learned by reading the sports page in the newspaper at age four as my parents would read it to me. I didn't start school until I was six probably because of the surgery; I was very shy around people, and my parents thought it was best if I would wait. Overall, it was a great decision and instead of being the very youngest in my class, I became almost the oldest.

Also, when we would go to athletic events, I would stay by my parents and actually watch the games unlike the other kids who would run around and not pay any attention. I would ask questions about why coaches did what they did. It seems strange but definitely explains why I do what I do today. I asked a lot of questions and was always fascinated by the "why" of sports like why is a certain person playing, why did the coach run this play, why is this team so good, etc. I have always asked a lot of questions (my wife gets irritated by that, and I'm sure my principals over the years would agree!) and have been a thinker on whatever I am involved with at the time.

I feel very fortunate to have grown up on a farm in small town Iowa. For as long as I can remember, I have been surrounded by people with an amazing work ethic. If something needed to be done, no matter how long it took, it got done. You didn't complain (at least not very often!) about getting up at the crack of dawn and working until the sun went down. It simply was what everyone did.

Many times, that work would get done with the cooperation of our neighbors. If someone needed help, there was always a neighbor just down the road willing and able to assist. For us, it was people like Art Wulfson, Kenny Grooters, or my dad's brother Roger who were there to help when it was needed. Whether it was baling hay or some other chore in small town Iowa, everyone worked together and got it done.

I loved everything about living on a farm. Whether it was milking cows, plowing or disking in the spring, walking beans in the summer, or harvesting in the fall, there was always something to do. There was plenty of space to work on the sports I loved as well. The pasture south of the acreage has thousands of extra rocks on it due to me constantly working on my baseball swing with rocks from the driveway! The basket on the garage also got plenty of use over the years as my makeshift hoop.

I was not alone growing up as I have two older brothers Larry and Steve, and an older sister Marianne who for the most part were out of the house during my childhood. All four of us as kids had issues when we were young that could have killed us, but somehow we survived. My issue was my appendicitis; Larry's heart stopped when he was getting his tonsils out, Marianne has numerous issues with diabetes, and Steve was born prematurely (only three pounds) and spent extra time in the hospital. He was so little he actually fell through an upstairs vent down to the main floor and somehow got off without a scratch!

5th grade with the family

Needless to say, there are many stories I could relay about troubles my siblings got into during their time at home. You wouldn't know it now, as all three of them are married with kids and grandkids and great role models for their whole family. Actually, they were role models for me growing up. All three had their "run-ins" with getting in trouble with the law, but I won't go into details here. I was always very observant growing up and vowed that I didn't want to make the same mistakes they made when I got older. My activities were more important than messing up and getting in trouble.

The family at my wedding

I learned a lot from my parents in how they handled my siblings' issues. Never did they blame others for what my siblings did. It was always stressed to take responsibility for your own actions. When my brother got a poor grade in PE because of not participating, my mom asked the teacher why it wasn't lower than that. When my sister got a speeding ticket shortly after her 16th birthday, my parents made her use all of her own money to pay the fine which was something the magistrate noted in court. We learned early to not make excuses and that we were accountable for our actions.

Dad was a Korean War Veteran who only went to school through eighth grade. However, he learned the value of hard work through his military time and through working numerous jobs. He passed that work ethic on to us kids. Dad has always been someone who didn't take any "crap!" He was a very quiet man (I think because mom doesn't give him a chance to speak!) but as my friend Todd Williams once said, "Your dad doesn't say much, but when he does, you know it's important."

Mom worked a couple of jobs when I was young, but for most of my childhood, she was home to get me breakfast in the morning, a snack after school (chocolate milkshakes!), and most importantly, to be at the many activities I was involved with at school. From both of my parents, I didn't get much "stuff," but I always got their time and attention which were much more important than material things.

During my childhood, my older sister Marianne was diagnosed with juvenile diabetes and has needed one or more insulin shots every day for the rest of her life since then. Mom has been a big part of Marianne's care and helped her through the already difficult teen years. Mom was also the main caregiver for my grandmother, who despite many ailments, was able to stay in her own home until her passing almost solely because of Mom's care and attention.

Despite numerous health issues, which included my dad's serious drinking problem after Korea (fortunately the move to the farm and away from a difficult job situation stopped that), a lack of money most of the time, the death of a grandchild at an early age, and four sometimes crazy kids, my parents stayed married for almost 64 years and were the epitome of perseverance. They knew there were always going to be tough times, but they kept pushing ahead with a positive attitude. Another lesson I've learned from my parents is that it has never been about them. Instead it has been about everyone around them. They truly define the word "service" and giving back to everyone.

I have mostly good memories of my elementary and middle school years. I was a good student and wanted to be liked and do what the teachers wanted. I was never a straight A student but worked hard and got the most out of my classes. I was blessed to have excellent teachers throughout my school years who were dedicated to kids and gave us the time we needed. I was lucky to have good role models to follow, and I have certainly patterned some of my teaching after the great teachers I had. I especially remember Mrs. Lentfer (I had her two straight years) and Mrs. Hunter who made learning fun and truly cared about each of their students. I am incredibly fortunate with the education I received from all of my teachers and undoubtedly they all are a part of why I have been in education for 30 years.

Up through 6th grade, I was a dedicated 4-H member, which included showing livestock at the Lyon County Fair. I actually loved being able to work with animals and groom them to be ready for the fair. One thing I didn't realize when I started was that after showing the cattle, someone would purchase my calf and slaughter it for food. I remember being devastated when I first found out that at a young age, I cared about animals and people and built relationships.

During my 5th grade year at the fair, my calf finished with a red ribbon, and we were dead last when the judges lined everyone up. I remember being very upset but was bound and determined to come back the next year with a blue ribbon calf and hopefully win one of the top prizes. Unfortunately, the next year came, and not only did I get a red ribbon again, but we finished dead last again! I clearly remember walking out of the ring, seeing Mom taking pictures, and telling her, "That's it, I'm done, I won't be back!" My competitive nature had struck, and I was done with 4-H!

Baseball was my favorite sport in elementary, and I idolized one of my coaches, Mark Schipper. We could have been related as he had a dark complexion, had similar physical features, and had a love of sports. He was a great coach. I remember him as being enthusiastic, having high expectations of

ALL of his players and making it fun to play baseball. His focus was on the team and on everyone improving on what they did each day. Doing our best was what mattered. Of course we tried to win, but he made it clear that the previously mentioned items were more important.

Coach Schipper's positive attitude and encouragement were huge for someone like me who was shy and wasn't that confident in what I was doing. Baseball built my self-worth and even though I made mistakes, I never felt like a failure. I always remember Coach Schipper called me AK, which stood for Ace Klaahsen since he thought I was so good at baseball. Wow, what an impact to have someone like that believe in you at such a young age. It wasn't as if he gave me anything. He would correct errors but made it positive and kept me eager to come back for more.

When Coach Schipper moved away and took a job in another town, it was really difficult to handle because of the impact he had. He went on to coach high school sports and eventually got out of the business of teaching and coaching, but I was so lucky to have him there in my early years because it shows the impact that one coach can have. I'll talk more about youth sports later, but if every youth athlete could have a coach like Coach Schipper, we would all be in a better place with sports. Interestingly, if you look at my coaching philosophy throughout my career, it closely matches the way Coach Schipper coached. Coaches today, take note because young eyes are watching every move you make. **What you are doing now could impact someone for a lifetime.**

Somehow, proper nutrition wasn't necessarily a strength of mine during those years. I was an incredibly picky eater (something I have definitely outgrown!), and had a few staple foods I loved to eat. I looked forward to coming home after school to have a chocolate malt from the blender. I'm almost ashamed to admit this (I'm sure mom has her head down reading this also) but during my sixth grade year, my noon lunch for almost every meal the entire year consisted of two glazed donuts from the George Bakery! Mrs. Fiihr was a teacher who required each student to clean his or her plate at lunch, and there was no way I could do that. My brother Steve had her as a teacher, and he really struggled with this, so I knew what was coming. I'm amazed my poor eating habits haven't done me in, but it showed my insecurity at the time with myself and my fear of failure. Mrs. Fiihr was an excellent teacher but unfortunately, her drive to make sure kids cleaned their plate had a very negative impact on many kids like Steve and me.

Until I reached high school, I was short, chunky, and had a dark complexion. When my oldest brother got married, I was so short I needed to stand on a box in order to be seen over the top of my sister who was in front of me wearing a bonnet! At a basketball game once, Mom was sitting by another parent new to the district. The parent saw me on the floor and said, "Who's that little Indian boy out there?" Mom replied, "That's my little Indian boy." I was a pretty typical middle school kid, but I did look different than many of my classmates.

Unfortunately, because of my appearance, I was the victim of bullying and harassment at times. Changing clothes in the locker room during PE was especially difficult. There were a couple of boys a year older than me who loved to pick on how I looked saying things like "What's that ring around your stomach? What reservation did you come from?" They would continue the harassment in the hallways and would threaten to beat me up if I ever said anything. I know I should have turned them in, but I feared for my safety. Also, I was very shy and kept a lot of things to myself, and I didn't want to bother anyone.

I think those incidents have turned me into someone who roots for the underdog and watches closely for kids who are picking on other kids. There is never an excuse for it. A favorite middle school phrase today is "We were just kidding around." Sorry, but there is never an excuse for bullying or harassment. I am constantly asking kids to speak up for themselves and to not let someone walk all over them. It can be a miserable life when others are putting you down.

Some of the best times growing up were gatherings with my uncles, aunts and cousins. I looked up (literally) to my uncles who all had gregarious personalities and loved to have fun. Every family gathering was full of laughs, and no one took himself or herself too seriously. It was a trick for all of us to have quick replies for my uncles as you never knew when they were going to try and prank you. Unfortunately, we never got together often enough, and I regret that we didn't have informal gatherings more often.

If there is a lesson to this, it would be to **cherish time with your family and do everything you can to meet when it's possible.** As the second youngest cousin on both sides, most of my cousins were older and with families as I was growing up so the chances to get together weren't the same. Today, it seems the only time we get together is for funerals, so take advantage of the times you have!

One of my favorite middle school teachers was math instructor Craig Van Kley. I loved math back then, and he made it fun, but there was also great learning as well. It probably didn't hurt that he was my basketball coach also. When we played, it was never about wins and losses. It was about learning, improving, and getting better. He was a very high-moral guy and a perfect role model for middle school students. In the classroom, he was always motivating us to learn more and not be afraid to fail. For example, he had us learn how to play chess even though it was difficult and very frustrating at first.

I've probably patterned much of my teaching and coaching after Coach Van

Kley. It shows the importance of kids having people in authority with great character. **Kids are always watching, and you never know when you might be influencing a student in a positive way.** He never swore, and we knew if he raised his voice, we must have done something really bad!

Middle school basketball was a blast. I played with my best friends, and we were quite good. We were the first George Middle School team to go unbeaten (18-0) throughout our middle school career! We played a fun style of run and gun basketball and Coach Van Kley motivated us to give it our best every day. It was sad to end my eighth grade year as I knew we would probably never have anything like that bond again.

Back then, there really weren't many AAU or travel teams for sports. There were, however, a few tournaments, but that was it. Our eighth grade team decided to play in a big tournament in Sioux Falls, South Dakota. We knew the competition would be tough, but we figured we would continue our streak. Unfortunately, we lost our first game! I was devastated, and it took me weeks to recover from that loss. Seems silly today, but it shows the bond we all had and how much it meant to us.

Another of my favorite middle school teachers was Terry McMillan who not only was the science teacher but the head boys' basketball coach as well. I looked forward to playing for him in high school so I paid extra attention in class. He kept his classes interesting, and the passion he showed in class and on the floor was something I admired. One day he got a little too passionate in class as he was lecturing up front when one of my classmates started falling asleep. Suddenly, Coach McMillan took a book and threw it at my classmate! Fortunately his arm wasn't the best, and he missed not only my classmate but also myself and everyone in class! Today, he probably would have had charges filed against him and would have lost his job, but back then, it was a fairly normal occurrence and no one was alarmed, but more on Coach McMillan in a second.

Fortunately I grew six inches before my freshmen year of high school and also got thinner so most of the harassment I received when I was younger because of my size stopped. I eagerly participated in baseball and basketball and also joined our local FFA (Future Farmers of America) Chapter. I was voted the Star Greenhand (long explanation) and also was our FFA creed speaker at district contest. I still remember the creed, "I believe in the future of farming with a faith born not of words but of deeds..."

My senior year, I became the president of our local chapter and had a close connection with our advisor, Dave Childress. He gave me a lot of freedom to do what I wanted as I worked on some new initiatives. He had confidence in me because of what I had shown before then and guided me but stayed out of my way. He trusted me to do the right things and valued my input even though

I was a student and he was a teacher. I will forever appreciate my experiences with him, and FFA helped me build confidence as I was pretty quiet and reserved socially, and participating and doing well gave me the belief I could do the same in other activities.

When parent-teacher conferences time came, they were set up where parents received a letter from a teacher to attend if their child received a D or F grade. The folks were surprised when they received a note from Mr. Childress asking them to visit him for conferences. Mom asked me what I had done wrong to receive a request like that. I claimed innocence and rightfully had no idea why he asked them to attend.

Mom went in for the conference, and Mr. Childress said he just wanted to thank them for having such a good kid and wanted to let them know how much he appreciated everything I had done for him and for the FFA/VoAg program. Mr. Childress also said he wanted me to stay on as FFA president for another year because I was doing such a good job, and he knew he never had to worry about anything getting done. What a simple thing Mr. Childress did but what an impact that had on my parents and on me! Many parents never receive a positive response from a teacher so think how much better relationships between schools and parents would be if teachers and coaches did more of this!

I wish kids today would try different activities like FFA, music, speech, etc. and move outside their comfort zone from time to time. We have too many young people who give up on something if they are not successful immediately and become unwilling to learn and grow from their experiences. I wish I had followed that advice in college, but more on that later…

I was blessed with some other outstanding high school teachers, with none better than Bev Hoing and Marcia Rosenboom, who taught English, Bill Hueser, who taught typing, and Mike Hoing, who taught social studies. Although I learned a great deal in each of their subjects whether it was grammar/punctuation (Mrs. H), principles of government (Mr. Hoing), typing skills (Mr. Hueser), or Shakespeare (Mrs. R), it was their structure, organization, high expectations, relatability to students, and passion that most stands out. I left their classes not only a better student but a better person as well!

By the time I got to high school, my brothers and sister were married and gone from the house, so I spent a lot of time helping my parents on the farm with the crops and taking care of animals. It was a lot of early mornings (Have you ever "walked" beans? Everyone needs that experience!) and late nights, but I loved it all. The peace and calm of being out in nature is a time I often wish I could go back to as I think back to those times. Life was a lot slower-paced than my life is now, and I try to remember those days when life gets hectic.

One of my favorite memories growing up was having dogs on the farm. We had a couple of dogs around who became part of our family. The dogs loved following us around on the farm, following the farm equipment, or riding in the pickup to the field. Eventually, we decided to try raising AKC registered Doberman puppies as we had a female, and my brother Larry who lived close and had a male. We did pretty well with those, and I enjoyed my first shot at being an entrepreneur.

Unfortunately, one summer, we lost not only our Doberman Cassy but also our husky Brandy who had been with us my whole life. One morning we got up and noticed the husky was not doing well, foaming at the mouth, and throwing up all over. We called our neighbor who was a vet, and he determined that the dog had been poisoned somehow, and unfortunately he died soon after. As we were wondering what happened, we noticed our Doberman showing the same symptoms. The vet came back and sure enough she had been poisoned as well. The Doberman gradually went downhill as well and despite our best efforts (I stayed up most of the night sitting by her, giving her water), she died too. It was devastating to lose both of them that close together!

We never found out exactly what happened but did get some information from some friends that there were people from George who were going to farms and stealing gas from tanks, and Dad had two tanks he used for tractors so he became a target. The thieves would bring poisoned meat with them to give to dogs so they wouldn't bark, and it would be easier to steal gas. The culprits were never caught but what a horrible action for anyone to consider, and it's always bothered me that we never caught who did that to our beloved animals.

Soon after that, my cousin Jack and his family had mostly lab puppies available so we went over, and I picked out a new dog. When we got home, Mom said I could name the dog and somehow out came "Buddy!" Buddy became a huge part of our lives and even after I left home for college and a career, Buddy would always go crazy when I came back! He was also a faithful outdoor friend for Dad when he would go outside and tinker around like he loved to do.

Unfortunately, farming in the 1980's was a difficult endeavor. I've always considered farming like trading on Wall Street. You are at the mercy of so many factors outside your control. Weather is one of those factors. I spent so much time watching the skies and watching the TV weather stations that I started to become intrigued by meteorology, and considered that as a possible career down the road. More to come on that in a bit as well...

Sports continued to be a main focus in high school. Because of my success in coaching basketball, most people assume I was a great basketball player, but unfortunately I was not. I spent more time watching others play than actually playing. I had an excellent freshman basketball season under Coach Bob Rabe.

Our team continued to have success, and I enjoyed being around my classmates.

Coach Rabe was a bit rough at times, but I loved playing for him. He was fair but firm and believed in each of us. One interesting fact we discovered was that he smoked. Obviously, he never smoked in front of us, but there were times when he would tell us we would be doing timed sprints, and suddenly when we would start, he would leave, and we wouldn't see him for a while. One time, we must have run for 15 minutes when suddenly he appeared and said, "Why are you guys still running?" We had a good laugh, and I loved the fact we learned a lot from Coach Rabe but also had a lot of fun.

Unfortunately, Coach McMillan and his wife Leanne, another great teacher and volleyball coach, moved to Orange City, and he got out of coaching to become an official. Interestingly, down the road, we ran into each other often as he officiated many of my games at Cherokee and even did one of our state games at Mason City! He became a hall of fame official, and I loved having him ref our games.

However, that went on to affect my basketball playing as the district hired Coach Stracke out of Nebraska to be the coach and his style was very different from my previous coaches. He was very knowledgeable and passionate about the game, but from the first meeting, he put fear into my mind and made me question my playing. Unfortunately, because of a wrist injury and a conflict with whether I wanted to play for the coach at the time, I did not play basketball my sophomore and junior years. I missed it and looking back, I regret that I probably used the injury as an excuse to not play when I should have "sucked it up" and given it a chance.

At the end of my junior year, I met with Coach Stracke and expressed my desire to play and worked that summer to get in shape to handle the rigors of the season. That summer, Coach Stracke announced his resignation and my senior year started with new co-coaches in basketball, Kelly Ryan and Richard HOOPS, and yes, that was his name! They brought new enthusiasm to my basketball career, but unfortunately, I did not play early in my senior year. I contemplated quitting, but Mom always said, **"If you start something, you don't quit it."** So I kept plugging away.

Unfortunately, one of my best friends Glenn Eben who was playing ahead of me tore his ACL, and I ended up starting every game the rest of the season. I had a season high of 18 points in a game with West Lyon and people were amazed that I actually could make 3's at times! We didn't have a great regular season but somehow beat West Lyon and Central Lyon in our first two tournament games after they had beaten us twice during the regular season. Unfortunately, 6'11" Darwin Klaassen (no relation) and his Little Rock team beat us by 10 and went on to state. I had a great senior basketball season because of not only the coaches, but also many of my best friends Tim Hamilton, Todd Geerdes, Jerry Schoo, Glenn Eben, and Jerry Kramer playing on the team. We weren't the greatest team but enjoyed our time together. Winning was important, but the journey was the real victory.

I was really lucky to have great friends in high school. We all had different backgrounds and different beliefs on things, but our love of sports definitely brought us together. Even today, over 30 years after graduation, we still keep in contact through social media and many still live in the George area. These friends all have great families and are very successful at what they do. I was also lucky to have many other boys (and girls) as friends and many were gained through activities at school. It is one of the reasons why I encourage kids to participate in activities because it is not only about the activity but the people you are around.

My senior year ended with my final baseball season. I had started almost every game since my freshmen year and was all-conference my senior year. Our numbers weren't very large, but we were overall pretty successful. We had a great senior season overall, losing only two regular season games. I was fortunate to be a first-team all-conference player and again played with my best friends.

We went into tournament play expecting a great run and started with Sanborn at home, a team we had beaten 22-2 earlier in the year. Sanborn's starting pitcher was a big left-handed kid named Daryl Damman who had a gregarious personality, but we were confident that we would win (more on Daryl later). Unfortunately, I picked that night to have the worst game of my career. I was 0-4 at the plate with three strikeouts and a costly error, and unfortunately we lost the game. Daryl beat us fair and square, and my athletic career was over.

Losing that game to Sanborn was devastating. It wasn't so much not making it to state even though we knew we had a chance. It was the realization that I would never play a competitive sport again. You hear stories about pro athletes and how hard the transition after ending their career is, and that was me in 1984. Mom tried to console me after the game ended, and I remember yelling at her to leave me alone. I didn't know how to handle it. Since then, with watching so many athletes end their careers in my sports, I have tried to help them ease the transition to a new way of life. I've always thought the kids I've coached recovered faster than I did at that time in my life.

CHAPTER 2

FIND YOUR RIGHT PATH; BE INVOLVED IN ACTIVITIES

Things Happen for a Reason

I attended college at Morningside College in Sioux City, Iowa. It was kind of a fluke that I ended up there. I had been accepted and planned to attend Buena Vista University in Storm Lake. I had never visited Morningside, but when my good friend Jerry Schoo decided to take a day from school in May to visit Morningside, I invited myself along and said I was a potential student as well. Jerry was checking on playing baseball there so I figured why not miss a day of school and check it out!

When we arrived, I was immediately drawn to the campus and had a special feeling that it was the place for me. The baseball coach mentioned I could play JV ball for them but would not receive a scholarship. However, the more I thought about it, the more I realized it might be time to end my sports career and focus on being a student. It was a big change for me because I had always been involved in sports and other activities throughout school, but at Morningside, I was just a student.

Looking back, I wish I had jumped into some extra curricular activities at college as I would have met more people and would have had a better overall experience. I have no thoughts that I would have been a star baseball player if I had tried out, but I think it was just accepting that I wasn't good enough to be a college player and hearing the coach say that I would never be good enough to play. It's why I tell kids today that they should try any activities they can when they are a freshmen-be it in high school or college. If it doesn't work out and they realize it isn't a good fit, it's fine to give it up. I don't want anyone to have the regrets I had about not giving it a shot when you have the opportunity.

Another problem at the beginning of my time at Morningside was my roommate. It was obvious that Morningside's philosophy was to match people up with totally different backgrounds. My roommate was from Spencer, but we had nothing else in common. He loved music and hated sports, he went to bed early and got up at 6 a.m. every day to work on his cleanliness and practice his instrument. I was the opposite of that. He was obsessed with keeping everything clean, and I was not. We did the best we could to make it work and survived the year, but then made a decision to switch roommates after the first year. I basically have not had any contact with him since. Fortunately, I had other George students on campus and ended up rooming with one of them the rest of my time in college.

I went to Morningside planning to be the next Tom Peterson (long time weatherman at KCAU TV in Sioux City who was tragically killed in an accident) and become a meteorologist. I always loved watching the weather and predicting what was going to happen. Unfortunately, I soon discovered the high amount of math and science needed to be a meteorologist, so I began with core classes at Morningside hoping to find the occupation for me.

Fortunately, one of the classes I took early was with a man named Sharon, Sharon Ocker, who along with my advisor, Dr. Marty Knepper (a woman!) guided me through the college years. Dr. Ocker had us do a number of presentations in class and one day after a class, asked what my major was. When I said I had no idea, he said, "You should consider teaching. You are very good at presenting in front of people!" Here I am, over 30 years later, still teaching away. Thanks, Dr. Ocker!

His encouragement started me on my way to a great career. **How many times could each of us help someone else out with just a tad bit more of encouragement?** His classes were very lively, and he was a big athletics supporter, something he constantly talked about in his classes. The fact that I went into teaching makes a lot of sense as teachers are like farmers because we grow things, we create situations where growth can happen, and that's something that's achieved and measured in a much different way than how normal success is judged.

Up to this time, my parents had been quite healthy, and I never had given thought to something happening to them. One day when I was at college, I received a call from Mom. After some small talk, she came out and casually mentioned that she had been tired lately, especially when going up the stairs. So, she went to the doctor and they ran tests. The doctors told her she needed a pacemaker. Wait, what?? Weren't pacemakers associated with old people? Are you going to die?

Mom assured me the doctors said they could get her back to health again. As she prepared for surgery, she was all about making sure everyone else was OK and not worried about her, and she would be fine. Fortunately, her surgery went well, and I distinctly remember her coming down the hall after surgery (obviously medicated) saying, "I'm fine, don't worry, it's all good." Yep, that's my mom - always thinking about everyone else!

During the time Mom was hospitalized, I was not married, and she tried repeatedly to find someone to pair me off with despite my laughing it off. One of her nurses was tall and pretty attractive, so of course Mom had to talk me up to her, especially when she found out the nurse wasn't married. The nurse and I had a good laugh about it and knew it wouldn't work, considering we were three hours apart in a world before the Internet and cell phones. Mom was always looking out for her kids!

The rest of my time at Morningside was nondescript. I was not a partier so I focused on my studies and went back to George most weekends to help my parents on the farm. My classes were fine, but it was mostly "let's get this over with" vs. having a great overall experience. I wish I could have those years over again.

I did fortunately have a great group of friends at Morningside, and one of those ended up to be my nemesis Daryl Damman. He was loud, sometimes overbearing, incredibly funny, and one of the best people I've ever met. We quickly got past our athletic history and discovered we had a ton in common. For some reason though, he always brought up that last game we played.

I graduated from Morningside in May of 1988. Daryl still had a semester to go, but we promised to stay in touch, and he said he was going back to Sanborn for the summer to work for the waste treatment plant in town. This was still the time before cell phones so keeping up was more difficult.

In June, I was helping my dad on the farm, and we had been in the field in the morning. When we went into the house for lunch, we turned the TV on. Remember that this was a time without cell phones or the Internet. The reporter's headline for the first story said, "Sanborn man killed at the city's waste treatment plant." I knew immediately it was Daryl. My heart sank as I waited for the rest of the story and unfortunately the details made my instinct correct. Ever since then, whenever I am watching the news and they start with someone from a particular city I know was killed, my heart drops a beat or two as I wonder if it is someone I know.

The funeral a few days later was what you would expect, very sad and a lot of talk about what could have been. I felt bad and although I had met the family, I really didn't know them well at all and didn't know what to say to them. They were so appreciative of me being there, but I felt I had let them down and should have connected earlier with them and their son. In the years after 1988, I have probably driven by the cemetery where Daryl is buried a hundred or more times, even stopping a couple times. Interestingly, the road to every place I have lived from George takes me past Sanborn so I think of Daryl every time I drive by that cemetery. I can't help but wonder what could have been for that big kid, what kind of husband, father, and worker he would have been. I'm sure he would have had a huge impact. It goes to show that **we can't take any of this life for**

granted!

Daryl epitomized what it meant to be passionate about life. He gave it everything he had no matter what he was doing and had fun with everything he did. Although I am not as free- spirited as he was, I have always tried to live with passion and enjoy what I do. **The energy with which we live not only makes our lives better, but also can have a huge impact on everyone around us. We owe it to ourselves to do that every day.**

That summer, I had my first "real" job. I was hired as the little league baseball coach in George. Although I had been around sports my whole life, this was the first time I had ever done any actual coaching. Baseball was my love, and I was thrilled to get started! I don't remember a lot about that experience except how enthusiastic the kids were. The time spent organizing practices, games, uniforms, the field, etc. was more than I had imagined. Although we didn't win a lot of games, the kids had fun, I had a lot of great comments from parents, and the players improved a lot. It made me want to get that first teaching job and get my coaching career started as well. This was a way for me to stay in athletics even though my playing career was over.

CHAPTER 3

SURROUND YOURSELF WITH GREAT PEOPLE

It's About People, Not Programs-Todd Whitaker

Unfortunately, by mid-summer of 1988, I didn't have a teaching/coaching job yet. I had interviewed a couple places but nothing had come of it. I was beginning to get discouraged and actually started making some backup plans in case nothing came up. Fortunately, the first week of July, I received a call from the Newell-Providence School District asking for me to come for an interview. Newell was about an hour and 45 minutes away from George and an easy trip to make. During the interview, everyone I met from Principal Phil Casey to secretaries Helen Harris and Eula Johnson and everyone in between, made me feel welcome and important. I was extremely nervous about the interview and knew how important it was to do well. One of the great things about living in small town Iowa is the fantastic people you meet and how everyone takes care of each other. Everyone during the interview made me feel like the most important person around.

When the call came that I got the job at Newell, a huge sense of relief came over me! Although I wouldn't be teaching in my major (the job was 6-10 English), I was not only thankful to get a chance to start teaching, but also was given three coaching jobs, one was middle school football, one was assistant boys' basketball, and the other was head baseball! There was a lot to do and not a lot of time to do it.

Fortunately, the person I replaced at Newell, Don Arends, had rented a small house just one block from school from an older couple, and they were looking to rent to a teacher again. He gave me their contact information, so I stopped by their house. Merlyn and June Bonde were the owners and lived a block away in a very nice corner house. As soon as I walked in, I knew this was going to be a good fit. They reminded me of my grandparents, so friendly, so open, and immediately offered me refreshments. We talked a bit and they offered to let me rent the house for $150 a month, payable the first of the month. They asked if that was OK, and they promised to keep it at that price for as long as I lived there.

Thus began eight years of walking to school every day, leaving my car in the garage, and stopping by the Bonde's the first of every month. It turned into me eating lunch or supper with the Bonde's almost every time I stopped unless they were out of town. They were great storytellers, and I know they loved the company as their kids and grandkids lived out of town. There were times I wanted to skip out, but every stop was a truly great experience for all three of us. I knew if something came up, I could go right to them for help, and I helped them out at times when they needed it. Merlyn and June were typical of all the fantastic people I met in Newell.

Needless to say, my first day with the Newell School got off to an interesting start. We had our first professional development meeting with staff on Monday in mid-August, and I was anxious to make a good first impression on everyone. I dressed up in my best white dress shirt, tie, and dress pants. I ended up getting to the meeting right at the start time of 8:00. When I walked in, I immediately got a big reaction from the staff as they were all in casual dress shorts and t-shirts. Immediately, I heard, "You must be the new guy," and "How come you are all dressed up?" Oops! Not the best way to start! Since then, I try to be in tune with what the dress code expectation is for staff on any occasion.

Fortunately, after that, the entire staff was great and welcomed me right in as a part of the group. I was overwhelmed with how to get started and what needed to be done. There were people at every corner ready to help. Phil Casey, my principal, lived right across the alley so we had an immediate connection.

Phil's boy, Matt was in my class and obviously, we saw each other a lot as neighbors. He always wondered why he couldn't call me Curt like his dad and other adults. I tried to explain to him that as his teacher, he had to call me Mr. Klaahsen like everyone else. Finally one day I told him, "When you graduate, you can call me whatever you want!" When Matt finally graduated, I was going through the reception line to meet the grads. When I got to Matt, he immediately said, "Curt, Curt, Curt...I can call you that now and you can't do anything about it"! I replied, "Thanks, dumb _ _ _ _; I've always wanted to call you that!"

I was fortunate at Newell to have great neighbors besides the Casey's, the Bauer's next door, the Waggoner's across the street, and the Bartsch's down the block. It doesn't get much better than small town Iowa where everybody knows your name, everybody waves at you when you pass them, and everyone takes time to slow down and have conversations. For the most part, I have been very fortunate with the neighbors I have had over the years. Immediately, I developed a bond with the social studies teacher next door, Jody Maske. We had a door between our two classrooms, and that door was used quite frequently my first year as I tried to figure out what I was doing.

Jody was the varsity girls' basketball coach at Newell so we hit it off immediately. The first thing that stood out what his passion for teaching, for coaching, but especially his passion for working with kids. It was clear kids loved his class and how he taught. He was especially helpful early in the year when

Principal Casey was diagnosed with cancer and missed much of the year. Jody became my mentor and made sure I kept my sanity throughout that first year. I wouldn't have made it through without him!

Jody was the announcer for the Newell football games, and I eventually became his spotter, basically writing down the number of the player who carried the ball, made tackles, etc. for both teams. We had a great time, and he always had a "scheme" where at least once a game, he would mention a tackler from the other team, but would use a number and a name of a player who wasn't on the roster! His favorite name was George Farquhar. We loved looking across the field at the opposing fans to see their reaction. Many times, people would reach for their programs wondering who "George Farquhar" was! I'll have more on Jody later.

My first coaching experience at Newell was as the middle school football coach. I hadn't played much football because George didn't have a team my senior year so it was a new experience. Newell's new head football coach was also a new teacher, Jeff Tiefenthaler, who had been a star football wide receiver and track runner at South Dakota State. He was a great athlete, and he would probably admit, pretty cocky and rightfully so. We became great friends during our time at Newell.

I leaned on "Tief" a lot for football, and I tried to run the pro-style offense he favored. Unfortunately, I was the only coach, and we did not have a lot of size. Trying to get my teaching organized during the day and then heading right to football practice was probably not the wisest thing I ever did. I found that as a new teacher trying to balance everything was difficult.

My very first official school coaching experience was a middle school football game against Albert City-Truesdale. I wanted to make a great impression on everyone and our kids were ready to go I thought. When we were warming up, I looked across the field and saw ACT's team. They had a young man that looked taller, bigger, and stronger than me! My kids also noticed and told me about it right away.

The game started and ACT immediately gave one young man the ball on every play, and you can imagine the results. The best coaching advice I had was, "We need to tackle him!" I clearly remember a player telling me after that advice, "But coach, he's bigger than us. What do we do?" Unfortunately, I didn't have an answer for that. They ended up winning 60-0 as the running back never came out of the game, and they probably gave it to him 30 times. We went on to lose every game that season although the kids were great to work with in the sport.

It was that fall that Bob Rehder, our head volleyball coach, approached me about replacing him. He had been trying to get out of the position for a number of years, and I'm sure he looked at me as a way to get out of it. I knew nothing about volleyball but was intrigued about the position. I had a number of his players in class and they were an enjoyable group. This would also get me out of middle school football so I told him I would think about it.

During the winter, I was the varsity assistant boys' basketball coach for head coach Phil Steger. I enjoyed my time working with this level and the coach and was able to coach the JV team as well. Phil did basically everything else and was an excellent X's and O's coach so it was a good learning experience. We weren't real successful, and we lost a couple of games to our rival Fonda. We had a decent record but ended up under .500.

I enjoyed my years teaching at Newell although there was a lot of prep time involved with teaching so many different English classes. My classroom was also in an upstairs room with no air conditioning and no windows. I think in my early years, I was too concerned about being a friend and being nice to the kids, and I wonder how much they actually learned. When you are only four or five years older than your students, it makes it more difficult. I will say we had a lot of fun in the classroom during those years and my teaching got better with experience.

As my first year wound down, the staff began hearing word that major changes were coming, and the school was looking at whole grade sharing with our neighboring district Fonda. The schools were huge rivals in athletics so needless to say, people in both towns were up in arms. Eventually, both schools decided to move forward with sharing. When the decision was made, I was informed that the schools wanted to put kids together immediately for the summer sports. In other words, my first head coaching position (baseball) was now going to be the very first Newell-Fonda combined activity. I was also told that I would be co-coaching the team with Fonda coach Paul Loos.

Paul and I fortunately got along great, and we had a pretty talented team. We knew our biggest task was going to be getting everyone on the same page working together. For the most part, the athletes got along fine and meshed well considering the circumstances. We really didn't have many upset parents, except for maybe one, who called Paul and me into his office one day. The parent complained about whom we were starting and asked why his son was not playing over our current left fielder who was from Fonda. We explained that our left fielder was hitting over .350 and had made a number of great plays in the field. Meanwhile, his son had been giving very little effort, and in fact had mooned his teammates at a recent practice while running laps. The parent (from Newell) then asked if we knew how many kids from Newell and how many from Fonda were in our starting line up. Paul and I looked at each other and said we had no idea as we didn't even think about that. We were going to play the best kids no matter what town.

Our baseball team played at the Metrodome

Since then, **I have always believed in playing the best players no matter what grade they were in, what town they were from, how much money their parents had, or anything else.** Which players would help us win the most is what matters. Coaches want to WIN. If you can help us win, you will play. Oh, and I forgot to mention that parent who talked to us was my superintendent in Newell. He actually was very contrite when we were done and was upset that his son had been messing around.

The next year, Coach Loos gave up baseball, and I was named the head coach. We never made it to state but had some excellent teams, winning a number of conference championships. In 1991, we had an incredibly talented team and our senior class, with basically the same group, won the state basketball and state golf titles earlier in the year, and we felt we could make it three in a row. I had a great admiration for this group as they graduated in May and could have taken the summer off to enjoy life before college but chose to stay with it.

We cruised through the season and reached the regional semifinal where we had to face a tough Laurens-Marathon team and their ace pitcher at their home field. We took a 2-0 lead into the late innings, and our best pitcher was cruising right along. Unfortunately, he hit a very rough spell and could not find the plate. I should have taken him out, but he was our best pitcher, and I felt he would come out of it.

Unfortunately, the walks continued, and I vividly remember a trip to the mound where I basically screamed at him with "You need to throw strikes!" What a profound statement! My pitcher replied, "I'm trying coach!" Needless to say, my speech didn't help as the opponents scored four runs and beat us 4-

2. I felt I let a lot of people down and have hopefully learned to **not let my emotions get the best of me in big games.**

Interestingly enough, today, some of these "kids" are highly successful coaches and great family men. One is a highly successful lawyer in Sioux Falls and sees my brother Larry frequently. I wish I had a do-over with that group as they were so talented and so much fun. There was certainly never a dull moment! Fortunately, because of this social media age we all live in, I am able to keep in contact with many of my former students and athletes through Facebook and Twitter. How cool it is to watch these young people mature into outstanding adults with jobs and families of their own!

Also that spring, Bob Rehder approached me again about taking the volleyball position. No one from Fonda wanted the position so the combined job was available. I knew Fonda had some good athletes so there were some good possibilities there. I took a class that summer and learned enough to feel I could take it on so my volleyball coaching career began in the summer of 1989. Success on the court was slow, but I grew to enjoy the sport greatly. The only bad part was the hot gyms. I was stubborn enough to wear a coat and tie to matches even when temperatures went through the roof.

During our first year of volleyball, we went 7-13-2, but improved steadily with 11-8 the next year and winning seasons every year after that. We were also able to win a number of conference championships despite competing against perennial power Schaller-Crestland and their fantastic coach, Marilyn Murra.

One of my last VB matches at NF was one of the most memorable, a district tournament match at Hinton. They had a better record than we did and also had the home court advantage. They had a large, loud, and obnoxious student section that was right behind our bench. During warm-ups, they were making very crude remarks to our players and to Coach Sievers, but we ignored everything. I heard a number talking about whom their next match would be against.

Our players came out on fire, and we blew them out in game one. We switched benches but their students continued to scream awful comments at our players. At one point, after a questionable call, I heard a loud "bull _ _ _ _" chant come out of the students! I turned to Kim and said, "Did I hear that right?" She heard the same thing!

We dominated game two and switched benches for game three. I had noticed someone talking to their students at times, but again, it kept up. The third game started, and I heard another chant. Suddenly, I looked behind me and the entire student section got up and started leaving! I asked Kim if they had play practice or something. We won the third game in a sweep and a much quieter gym. I found out later that the principal from Hinton had talked repeatedly to the students and there were many kids involved, not just a few. He had warned all of the students to clean it up, or they would be removed. Immediately after that, the last chant came out and the principal sent them on their way.

Interestingly enough, I caught wind the next day that the principal was catching a bunch of heat from parents for what he did. I emailed him and gave my support and then sent an email of what happened and how much I supported what the principal did. I found out later that nothing happened to the principal because of his actions, and I was thankful for that. It's very sad that parents defended the actions of the students at that match. Granted, you are always better off discipling individuals and not a whole group like that as certainly some students had to leave who weren't doing anything. However, at some point, when it's hard to differentiate who is causing problems and who is not, something had to be done.

When the match ended and we were getting ready to leave, I had a player tell me that a lot of their students were in the parking lot close to the bus. We waited until all the players were done in the locker room and went out to the bus together. We had planned to stop at a convenience store at the outskirts of Hinton, and when our bus started getting closer, I saw a huge group of kids standing outside the store. I quickly told the driver to keep going, because we weren't stopping! As we drove past, the ENTIRE GROUP gave us a "one finger" salute...I don't need to tell you which finger it was. How classy! I told the kids their students were just telling us we were #1, and we should be thankful!

It goes to show what we try to talk about with kids. **You have to control what you can control and not worry about anything else. If we are constantly bothered by the actions of others, it is bound to make life worse, and usually there is little we can do to change others' attitude.**

We never made it to state in volleyball, but it was a great experience. Many of the athletes played basketball and volleyball and were in my class, so a great bond was created. I had fantastic assistants (two were named Kim Sievers!) and players who did whatever I asked.

Early in my years at Newell, I jumped on board with two pieces of technology that we all take for granted today, the Internet and satellite TV. I remember being one of the first people in town to have Internet, although it was nothing like we have today. My installer ended up to be the orchestra teacher at Cherokee and a future colleague. Internet was very frustrating back then because it was connected directly to the phone so whenever someone called me, I was immediately kicked off the Internet! As you can imagine, it was also VERY slow, but it definitely changed the way we lived and the way we taught school.

In the early 1990's, there were a number of people who had large satellites to gain access to more television channels. Otherwise you had local channels and that was it. I was intrigued by the possibilities of satellite TV, so in the mid 1990's, I signed up for a new system of satellite TV called Direct TV. It gave me many more channels to watch although it seemed like a large risk at the time. I have basically been with them since. It's funny to think back now how we take the Internet and satellite TV for granted when it seemed so strange not that long ago.

Although I was not married during my time at Newell, for a number of years in the summer, I was "dad" for a week each summer for two of my nephews, Kevin and Kory, who would stay with me and attend basketball camp at Buena Vista in Storm Lake. The boys were becoming teenagers during this time, and for a few years, they brought a couple of their friends along. This was during the time I was coaching baseball so days were busy with running them to Storm Lake and then heading to the baseball field at night. I also drove the bus for baseball trips on the road and had to get the field ready at home, so there was never a dull moment! My NF players treated them tremendously well, and they turned into excellent batboys for the team.

Fortunately, they were well behaved (most of the time) although they liked to stay up late and eat snacks in their beds. One year, I asked them very clearly to not have food in the beds, especially sunflower seeds. Low and behold, after they left, there were sunflower seeds (and other surprises!) everywhere! Those were memorable times with the nephews though. They are great kids who loved sports, and it gave me a chance to help them with sports, since I did not have kids of my own. I was lucky to watch their middle school and high school athletic careers with great pride. Both are now outstanding young adults with great careers (Kevin has 3 great kids of his own now), and I'm glad to have survived having them on my own for those weeks in the summer.

CHAPTER 4

THE BEGINNING OF A NEW PASSION

Find Your Passion

Another coaching change involved my basketball situation. With Newell and Fonda going together, the Fonda coach was chosen as the head boys' basketball coach and the Newell coach as his assistant. They did add a freshmen team, and I figured I would be that coach. At that time, Coach Maske started discussions with me about joining the girls' basketball program. Iowa girls still played 6 on 6 at that time (anyone know the rules on that?), and he was looking for someone to work with his guards. I would be the freshmen coach but also have the responsibility of running the defense.

Obviously, the boys were looking for a freshmen coach as well, so I had the choice to either stay with the boys' program or jump to the girls'. Because of the persuasive skills of Coach Maske, and the ability to be a big part of the varsity team, I chose the girls' program. 26 years later, I'm still going strong with girls' basketball! I have never regretted my choice, except maybe two years later when our Newell-Fonda boys won the state title, and the freshmen coach sat on the bench, spoke at the assemblies, and got to be along for the ride.

The seven years coaching with Jody were some of the best times of my life. I spent hundreds of hours at his house watching tapes but also being entertained by his saintly wife Deb, kids Josh and Niki, and their ever-present dogs. That was my introduction also to two drinks that I partook in frequently, vodka sours and Diet Pepsi. I used to drink all Mountain Dew, but somehow learned to like diet pop!

The tape watching nights at the Maske house were always a blast. We had the bad habit of finding funny things that happened on tape and then would rewind them over and over again. Unfortunately, Jody's technical skills were not that strong so many of our laughs came from him trying to work the old-time VCR player!

On the nights we had home games, the Maskes would host their family and friends for a social gathering which also became known as a rehashing of the night's game. Jody's dad was an ex-coach, so the strategy of the NF coaches was always a big topic of discussion. There was never a dull moment as people like the Nielands and the Lymans were there and the laughs were plenty.

One of the most memorable times I had coaching basketball with the NF girls was after a game at Pocahontas. We had heard that the weather could worsen throughout the evening, but we had no reason to be too concerned. The boys' game ended, and we proceeded to hit the road. Pocahontas was no longer than a half hour trip to Newell so getting home wouldn't be a problem. Unfortunately, as we headed out of town, a crazy blizzard hit Pocahontas with some light snow but very high winds, which made driving very difficult. We were only a couple of miles out of town and visibility was at zero. We thought about turning around but that was basically impossible so we kept going slowly. We did call the school and made sure the boys' bus stayed where they were.

Our fantastic bus driver, Paul Bjorklund, was having a tough time seeing, so coach Maske and I looked out the windows on both sides and tried to navigate Paul between the white and yellow lines on the road although that was very difficult. It was a lot of "left Paul, a little more right, Paul" for a long stretch. We found out during the trip that one of our cheerleaders was starting to have a panic attack and possibly some breathing issues. She had issues previously so that just added to the concern on the bus. She did finally get calmed down and made it through the trip fine.

We eventually made it to our turn to go west on Hwy 4 to head toward Fonda. After a couple of miles, we noticed some taillights ahead. When we got closer, we noticed a car in the ditch. Paul stopped the bus, and Jody and I got out to investigate. We found a lady in her car with the door partially open, literally freezing to death! She had driven into the ditch, the door had popped open, and she couldn't get it closed. We got the door open far enough to get the lady out and helped her on the bus. She was shivering but so thankful we came by! Who knows what would have happened if we had not come by when we did.

We kept going and eventually got to Fonda. We dropped off some kids, but obviously a number of us had to get to Newell yet which was still about seven miles away. After a discussion with one of our parents, it was decided to take the rest of the team and coaches to their house, and we stayed overnight. I ended up sleeping on a floor. It was not the best sleep but at least we were safe. The weather improved greatly overnight, and we were able to make it back to Newell but not without creating a lifetime memory.

It was during these times that we created a key concept for successful teams that we called the "fun factor." The most successful programs seemed to be having more fun than anyone else. Certainly winning was part of that. However, being part of a family atmosphere where everyone was accountable to each other added to the fun. We were very serious about everything we did but took time to enjoy the process and the people we were with as well. **Finding the "fun" in everything we did was a philosophy I have tried to carry with me into my teaching and coaching.**

One of Jody's strengths was **trusting in his assistants to do their job, and he gave us the freedom to make decisions and give input.** Before and after every game, along with every halftime, once he was done talking to the team, he let me give my thoughts. I felt like a valuable part of the team and that people cared what I said. I have always kept the same philosophy with my assistants. Coach Maske helped me grow tremendously as a coach and made me ready to be a head coach when the opportunity arose.

Jody's teams had excellent success before I arrived, and we were able to continue that success. One of our toughest years was during the 1993-94 season which ended up to be the last year of 6 on 6 basketball in Iowa. Jody was a 6 on 6 aficionado and was devastated that the game he had worked so hard on perfecting was being taken away. We were bound and determined to make it to state and celebrate the last year of 6 on 6 in style. Our team that year was our best with high-scoring, excellent defense, great chemistry crew and a team we felt could win the whole thing. We cruised through the regular season and made the regional final, which was one game away from the state tournament.

The regional final was one of the most heartbreaking games of my career. The team we played employed a strategy of letting one of our forwards shoot every time she got it. Our philosophy of offense was "if you are open, shoot the ball." Unfortunately, our player (normally a great shooter) had an off game and could not hit anything. Our defense was also not as good as usual, and we ended up losing a close game.

Devastated would not be strong enough to explain my emotions after that game. I felt we had let so many people down and that it wasn't fair that we had come up short. How could this great group of players and coaches be denied something they had so richly earned throughout the year with such great effort? Being unmarried at the time, I went home alone to my house to sulk. I remember not sleeping that night and wondering if I should continue to coach. Making it to state was my main goal, and not making it made me and the team a failure.

The next day, I heard my doorbell ring, and it was Coach Maske. He came in, and we commiserated about the game, the season, and our future. All I remember was his amazing attitude. He reminded me why we coach, how winning and losing doesn't determine whether we are successful or not, and the large impact we have on kids. He asked if I coach only to win games. Of course, I answered no, but my attitude showed that maybe I did.

Although the loss still hurt, I felt so much better going forward and since then have tried to put losses in perspective. We might feel that it is not "fair" sometimes when we lose a game, but other teams work hard and care as much as we do. Sometimes winning is not "meant to be." **If you enjoy the journey along the way, you can survive any disappointments that come along.**

Once we moved on from the disappointment, our next step was trying to figure out the future. The game of basketball was moving to 5 on 5, when both of us were huge supporters of 6 on 6. I think we both questioned whether to continue or to give it up. Because of the items I mentioned earlier, we decided to jump head first into the new game. Going into that new endeavor, I think we believed we would be as successful as we were in the 6 on 6 game. We both had some 5 on 5 experience, and we both were passionate about the game. Practice started and unfortunately, things just didn't mesh as we'd hoped. We won some games before Christmas break, but we were boring to watch and games were in our terms "ugly."

Over break at a meeting, Jody and I decided the heck with what we had been doing at this point. We were going to turn into a fast breaking, full-court pressing play for 32 minutes basketball team and let the chips fall where they may. That decision turned out to be the best thing we ever did! Suddenly, wins started coming, fan support grew, and the buzz around our program increased. Although we came up short for the state tournament that year, we knew better days were ahead.

The following season (1996-97) culminated in our first ever state tournament appearance. The road to state was difficult. We won a regional semi-final when officials didn't notice we had six players on the floor for a short time, and we somehow got her off the floor. However, we had unbelievable fan support (people were lined up an hour or more before most games), and making it to state and seeing the reaction of everyone was the thrill of a lifetime!

That first state experience was memorable as we played our archrival Pomeroy- Palmer in round one and got down 15 points going into the fourth quarter. Behind an incredible performance by our point guard and an unrelenting full court press, we pulled the game out 67-64. Two days later, we played a towering Winfield-Mount Union team who again got us down big going into the last quarter. Once again, we made a huge comeback and tied the game with 30 seconds left. Unfortunately, WMU's Linda Lappe (later to become the head women's coach at Colorado) broke our hearts by hitting a jumper to win the game. WMU went on to win the championship by over 30 points, and we knew that could have been us.

It was another devastating way to end the season. We thought it was our time, but it wasn't meant to be. Again, Coach Maske was a pillar of strength and class for our team and our fans. That night, we went back to the motel, and he promised one loss wasn't going to define the season and that we were going to enjoy the rest of the week. That was a special group of kids, and Jody always had the big picture in mind. No matter how upset we were as coaches at losing, the team needed to leave with great memories, and he made sure that happened the rest of the week. Unfortunately, I have had too many incredibly difficult

Our first Newell-Fonda appearance at state

losses to end seasons, and I have tried to emulate how Coach Maske dealt with those losses.

The next year was another transition year. We found out that our Bo-Coon conference would be disbanding, and we would join the Twin Lakes conference. We wanted to go out on top and had a great season going unbeaten and rolling to another state appearance. Again, we thought it was our turn and felt confident going into state.

That confidence quickly left as Treynor, our opponent, was bigger, stronger, and tougher than us and beat us handily. We were very disappointed, but it wasn't like the previous year and how close we were to winning. We knew we had a great group coming back again, and we would have a chance to win the whole thing. Little did I know at the time that it would be my last basketball game for Newell-Fonda.

The spring of 1998 came, and I began to have thoughts of what my future should look like. I had frequently looked at want ads for teaching openings and had even applied for a couple of possibilities during my time at Newell-Fonda. I had zero reasons to move on but wanted to keep my options open. So in early April, an ad appeared in the *Des Moines Register* for an opening in Atlantic, which was a 3A school in Southwest Iowa. The opening was for language arts teaching, head volleyball, and head girls' basketball along with freshmen baseball. By this time, I was feeling a strong passion to be a head girls' basketball coach. This was probably a surprise to most people considering I was a head volleyball and baseball coach at NF. Since Atlantic was a much larger school and I had only been an assistant at a 1A school, I didn't expect much to come from my application, but I decided to send it in anyway.

When June arrived, I had not heard anything from Atlantic, and I assumed they had hired someone for the positions. I signed my Newell-Fonda contracts, worked hard with my baseball team, and planned for summer camps. Then suddenly in the second week of June, I received a call from Atlantic Schools wondering if I was still interested in a position with their school as they were just starting to look through the applications. Of course I said sure, and a couple days later, I received another call asking if I could come down to interview ASAP. I scheduled the interview for shortly thereafter, still not thinking anything would come of it.

When I got to Atlantic, the first two people I met with were principal Roger Herring and Athletic Director/Assistant principal Bob Sweeney. My meeting with Roger went well, and I learned that part of my teaching job would include being in charge of the yearbook. Considering I had no experience with a yearbook, I knew that would be an interesting challenge. However, the school was brand new, the gym was amazing, and I was beginning to envision myself being a "Trojann" (their nickname for girl athletes because boys were Trojans; very interesting name!)

When I met with Bob, I was immediately impressed with his confidence and his positive attitude about the position. I was still thinking that I probably wouldn't get the job because of too much inexperience but wanted to see what would happen. One of his big questions was, "Why should we hire a small school assistant for a 3A school?" I knew that question was coming so I tried to channel my best example, Jody Maske who said, "We will work hard, have a great attitude, and have fun." I stressed my ability to work with kids, parents, administrators, etc. and my belief that we would be successful and do this together. Something must have hit home because from the beginning, I felt like Bob was on my side and was excited about everything I was saying. Both the volleyball and basketball positions were open, and I definitely thought because of my experience that the jobs could be mine.

I went back to Newell and waited for word from Atlantic. Within a day, I received a call from Mr. Sweeney telling me the teaching job was mine, and I had my pick of either head volleyball or head girls' basketball coach, as they wanted to hire another teacher to coach the sport I didn't choose. Wow! I had to decide whether to leave my great life at Newell behind, and if I did, which sport would I coach?

It was an agonizing decision because there were so many positives at Newell with great people, great kids, and great living conditions, but I felt it was time for a new challenge. Probably the people that needed the most convincing were my parents as I would now be three hours away from home vs. an hour and 45 minutes. They lived in the same town their whole lives so stability was and still is everything to them. Eventually, they understood and were a big help in the moving process.

I also had a decision to make in deciding whether I should coach volleyball or basketball. Not many people know that I had a choice in the matter and most would have been surprised at my choice based on my history. It really was an easy decision because basketball had become a true passion, and I wanted a chance to lead my own program and continue to build on what I had learned from Jody.

After I decided to take the Atlantic job, the first thing I did was let everyone at Newell know. I started with the administration. I had already signed a contract with Newell-Fonda so I knew there was a chance they would not let me out of my positions. I visited with our superintendent, Merle Boerner, and he pulled out my contracts. His first comment was, "Holy crap; you do a lot for our district. What extra can I pay you to stay?" We both had a good laugh about that, and I knew that was not possible. He did tell me that I had to pay for the advertising for my position which would be around $400, and they would get moving as soon as possible. There were some nervous days after that wondering whether I would be able to leave, but fortunately a replacement was found.

I was coaching baseball at the time, so I knew I had to get the word out as quickly as possible and with the right people. I found my friends and let them know I was leaving and then decided to let my baseball team know at practice that night. I knew I wouldn't be able to get to all of the girls I coached but knew the news would spread quickly. Fortunately, this was the time before social media and cell phones so I could keep it pretty quiet until I let the team know.

Our baseball practice ended up in the Fonda gym because of weather, so after practice, I sat the team down and let them know. This was my first experience with letting people down with an announcement like that, and I struggled with the right words to say. I got through it the best I could, but I could tell the boys were shocked. They showed little emotion, however, other than being quiet. Word spread quickly and in the days ahead, I saw most of the volleyball and basketball players at baseball games or around town. The biggest question of course was "Why are you leaving?" It was incredibly hard leaving such a great group of kids. However, someone once told me, **"If you build your program right and do the right things, you will always leave great kids."** This just felt like the right move and I was not married, so the decision to move on got easier over time.

I was so blessed to start my career at Newell-Fonda with great people who went out of their way to help others, mentors who taught me so many life lessons, and players who showed what hard work and perseverance could do. It was and still is small town Iowa at its finest! Newell-Fonda continues to be one of the premier small schools in Iowa and it's because of the quality of people that live there! It was a continuation of what I had experienced at George, but it was time to move on to Atlant

CHAPTER 5

BE A MENTOR TO OTHERS

Live Your Life Without Fear

One of the first people I contacted in Atlantic after getting the job was the former head coach, Don Jenkins. Don was a legend in girls' basketball circles, a hall of famer, and I was very nervous about getting his thoughts about the status of the program. Here I was, a 1A assistant replacing a hall of famer! I wanted to know what I was getting into and why he had left. Coach Jenkins couldn't have been nicer on the phone. He was very honest and said much of why he was getting out was because of parent issues. This was something I really hadn't dealt with at Newell-Fonda. He filled me in on the returning players and got me contact information about the returning assistants, Dick Casady and Kathy Sarasio. He said when I got to Atlantic to look him up.

About a week later, I headed to the school in Atlantic and Coach Jenkins happened to be there. He asked me about summer plans, and I mentioned I didn't have a house yet but was coming down shortly to put on a camp. Don asked where I was staying, and I mentioned a local motel. He said, "The hell you are! You are staying with my wife Nancy and me."

Wow! Here was someone whose job I was taking and whose experience was much more extensive than mine going out of his way to help me out and make sure I was successful. Don, his wife Nancy (a teacher as well), and son Alan took me in for the week and gave me a place to sleep, plenty of meals, and a ton of stories and laughs to make me feel like I was welcome. I picked his brain as much as possible about his coaching philosophy, and I am forever grateful for his willingness to share. I have tried to follow his example and be a mentor to anyone who has asked for my assistance.

During my time in Atlantic, Don and I and some of his SW Iowa friends took various trips that were many times basketball-related but turned into great learning experiences for me in many ways. I believe Don knew someone in every town in SW Iowa and also knew the location of many of what I will call "fine establishments" in these towns. They were all legal establishments but to say I had some eye-opening experiences with that group would be an understatement!

Another example of someone who helped mentor me through my beginning at Atlantic was Mary Turner. Mary was a long-time language arts teacher and former yearbook advisor. The yearbook was something I was required to take on with my teaching job. I literally knew nothing about the yearbook and particularly the darkroom and developing pictures (yes, we still did that back then!) were foreign to me.

Before school started, I connected with Mary, and she couldn't have been more helpful with giving me at least an idea of what I was doing with the yearbook. Her patience never wavered despite my constant questions. The actual yearbook person I was replacing was out of town and hadn't cleaned out her room yet so Mary's help was invaluable.

I was able to find a house in Atlantic, get moved, and got ready for the new school year. That summer, coaches were still limited to ten contact days with players, so I had very little time to implement a lot of major changes that the players weren't used to. We wanted to play like Newell-Fonda played with a fast break offense and pressure defense. My new players had played half-court offense and man-to-man defense. Fortunately, my new players had a great work ethic and a great attitude, so we had a lot of fun getting ready for the new season. I'm sure Coach Casady and Coach Sarasio had some doubts about what the heck we were doing, but they jumped in with both feet and supported me in whatever was needed to get done. I knew our team had a ways to go, but I was excited for the season to get started.

My first day of school in Atlantic was quite interesting. When I got to my room, the person I replaced was in the room finally starting to pick up her "stuff." She had a ton of files and was going through each of those. My very first class happened to be my yearbook class so I was quite nervous to start. The person I replaced stayed in the room (despite asking her to come back after school) and literally interrupted class three times to ask me questions about different things. Clearly, she wanted to see how things would go and make her presence known. In many ways, I felt bad for her, as it appeared she also had trouble giving up her job to retirement. I finally had to call Mr. Herring to come down and ask her to come back later. She finally left but not without leaving quite an impression!

My other classes at Atlantic were sophomore and junior English classes. Back then, the accelerated group (basically A and B students) took honors English, so basically, the classes I had were students with low B's and under. Needless to say, I had a number of students who were basically in the class to pass and get a credit and had no interest in following instructions or making class a great place of learning. I'm not sure my teaching those years was the best for those groups so we all struggled to learn.

Unfortunately, I had some tough incidents with students that I could have handled better. As a young teacher, I was pretty impatient, and I'm sure kids picked up on that. This was not a good approach with the most difficult students I had during this time. There were rumors from other teachers of drug use by some of those students and none of my strategies with them seemed to work.

In the two years I lived in Atlantic, I had three serious incidents at my house. No one was ever determined to have perpetrated those incidents, but I'm pretty certain they were all caused by students I had. The first one was fairly minor. I was sitting in my living room one night when I heard a bunch of firecrackers going off right outside my front door. As I ran to the door, the firecrackers had ended, but my doormat was on fire! I quickly put the fire out and did not see anyone outside who might have done it.

Later on, I had a much more serious incident. I was again sitting at home watching TV and sitting in a chair next to my beautiful plate glass front window when suddenly CRASH! The window shattered, and there was a brick lying at my feet! After overcoming the shock and realizing what happened, I ran to the door and saw a car squealing away up the hill. I could not see anything about the car. When the police came, they said to keep my ears open at school as they were certain it was probably a student.

The next day, I pulled many of my players aside and asked them to stay alert for anything they may hear at school. Right after lunch, two of my players came to me and said that two of my students had bragged at lunch about what they had done. When I talked to my principals and the police again, they said that was hearsay and that without a confession, the students' bragging was not admissible.

Those two students had always been troublemakers, and it grew worse in the days ahead. Both were totally disrespectful and said repeatedly, "You can't do anything to me" while laughing in my face. One day, I finally had enough and kept them both after class. After shutting the door, I said, "Gentlemen, we all know what you did to my house, and you'll probably get away with it. But if something happens again, you'd better be home as I am driving directly to your house, and if you aren't home, your parents better know where you are, and you'd better have a great alibi or the police will be visiting with you. Also, if your attitude in class doesn't change, you will be out permanently with no credit. Thanks and you may leave now." This was probably pretty risky on my part, but I had had enough, and didn't really care at that point. Interestingly, their behaviors got much better, and one of them ended up leaving school not too long after that because of a drug issue. A friend of theirs told me later that they admitted to being high the night of the incident and weren't sure why they had done it but knew where I lived and acted impulsively.

During my second year at Atlantic, I spoiled myself and bought a hot tub. I had a nice, secluded back yard with plenty of room so I was glad to put it to use. I used it a fair amount, and it was securely locked, so you would think all was well. Unfortunately, one weekend, I went back to George to visit my parents. When I drove in my driveway, I noticed a couple of beer cans lying close to the hot tub. When I walked toward it, I immediately saw that the straps with the locks on it had been cut. When I opened the lid, the water literally looked like a muddy river so clearly a lot of people had used that hot tub during the weekend. I checked with my next-door neighbors. One had been out of town all weekend, and the other (with a teenage daughter who was kind of a rebel) said they were home but hadn't seen anything. Humm...considering it had to be a lot of people who had used the hot tub, and my neighbors across the street had seen a lot of people at my next-door neighbor's house, it didn't take much to figure out what happened. Unfortunately, those incidents took away from a house and neighborhood in Atlantic that I really liked but did help make my decision to move on from Atlantic easier. More on that later...

Fortunately, when basketball season started, I was able to be surrounded by great young people and coaches who clearly had learned much from Coach Jenkins and were easy to work with in the program. We had high expectations going into the season but knew with a total change in style, there would be some tough moments.

Our first game was at home against perennial power Harlan. I don't remember the score at the end of a quarter, but all I remember was a track meet as both teams scored at will, both were running and pressing, and everyone was out of breath, which was exactly the way we wanted to play. Unfortunately, we couldn't keep the momentum going and lost 83-52, but after the game, everyone I saw was excited about the way we played. It was the first game of my career where the boys didn't play at the same place as the girls, so that was hard to get used to. Fortunately, Atlantic did a great job of supporting all of their activities!

The season overall went quite smoothly with few issues. One thing that became an issue for a short time was a disagreement with my assistant, Coach Casady. His daughter (great kid!), played on the team, started some games, and came off the bench some. Her playing time varied as she at times struggled to fit into our up-tempo style.

During one game, we were playing at Carroll Kuemper, and the coach's daughter did not play much. In fact, I remember having to get on her a bit. I began to notice that Coach Casady stopped coaching and tended to be quite irritated. I asked him a couple of times what was wrong and did not get an answer. The game ended, and we lost by a big margin. Neither of us said a word on the way home.

When we got back to Atlantic, I asked Coach Casady to meet in our office. We had a very difficult talk about the situation and both agreed we should have handled it a lot better. From that point forward, he did an amazing job for me, and we were great friends during our time in Atlantic. It definitely gave me more of a perspective on what parents go through when their kids aren't playing and how much harder it is when the parent is coaching. I've tried to have empathy during talks with parents and coaches and even though we won't always agree, discussions like this with no yelling should make things better. Coach Casady's daughter did not finishing her senior year because of some health issues which probably made it easier for him and myself. We ended up starting with winning 6-2 but then fell off at the end of the year, winning only two of our last 11 games to finish 8-11. However, our leading scorers were underclassmen and with an excellent eighth grade class coming on board, we knew our best days were ahead.

I spent a lot of time at the state tournament in Des Moines in 1997. Our local radio station KJAN and Jim Field, it's fantastic sportscaster, broadcasted every game at state. I'm not sure how it started, but he asked if I wanted to be his "color man" whenever I was down at state. I've enjoyed being on the radio so I agreed to help when I was there. Atlantic was a little over an hour from Des Moines so I went down after school and actually took a couple of personal days to go down as well. I had a blast, Jim was a pro's pro, and it was great to see the other side of a sports contest. I have always had a great respect for the media and have been blessed to have outstanding coverage of my teams wherever I have been.

Jim Field of KJAN & I at state in 1997

Interestingly enough, one of the games I broadcasted in 1997 was the 1A championship game. One of the participants was Newell-Fonda. Yep, that would have been me sitting on the bench as an assistant if I had stayed. I must admit that I definitely had mixed feelings about being there. I was thrilled for Jody and the kids but also had a small bit of regret that I wasn't part of it. They came up short in a close game, and I felt terrible for my great friend and the entire team, but it was great to see them have continued success.

CHAPTER 6

HELP OUT WHERE NEEDED

Be a Servant Leader

That spring, Anita, a small town just east of Atlantic was looking for a head baseball coach for the summer. When I saw the opening, I immediately considered applying; somewhat in spite for not being considered for the head baseball position, but mostly because I felt I would do a good job and could help a neighboring school out in a difficult situation. I still was not married at the time, was used to coaching all the time, and still enjoyed baseball so it made the decision even easier.

Originally, there was a thought that the head baseball position would be open in Atlantic, and I was very interested in that at the time. However, it was decided to stay with the current coach, which did frustrate me a bit. When I talked to Mr. Sweeney about it, he definitely was against me applying. It was hard to go against his wishes, but ultimately he said it was my decision. When I contacted Anita, they were interested so I went over to visit with their administration. They quickly offered me the position, and I decided to accept.

It would be unfair to label that team the Bad News Bears, but we were probably pretty close. We only won a handful of games, and the kids were pretty undisciplined and lacked a lot of skills. I enjoyed being around the team, and they worked hard for me, but clearly it was a tough season. After the season, I let them know I was only a one-year coach. I thought my helping out other schools was done. I was wrong!

During that summer, I received a call from someone associated with the Griswold School District, which was a small school about 15 minutes south of Atlantic. They were desperately looking for someone to coach their volleyball team. They had a young assistant in Chris Jahnke and wanted to pair someone with him for the upcoming volleyball season to officiate. For the first time in seven years, even though I had not coached volleyball in my first year at Atlantic, I became volleyball official with Coach Jenkins. That was certainly a strange sight with two head coaches walking into gyms with striped shirts. I'm not sure why I didn't take any pictures of this!

After visiting with the person from Griswold and giving it a lot of thought, I decided to contact the district about their volleyball position. Mr. Sweeney, once again, was not real thrilled, but supported my decision. I interviewed shortly after that and was given the position. It was a difficult season. We had a lot of experience, but played in a tough conference and struggled to win many matches. As always, I gave 100% effort and felt like I helped their kids out a great deal. However, I felt some resentment from Atlantic people who felt I should have been loyal to them, even though I couldn't do anything with our basketball players in the fall. I think it was a combination of me helping out both Anita and Griswold that seemed to be the problem. Even though our teams didn't compete in the same conference, I think a lot of people questioned my loyalty to Atlantic which was never an issue to me.

During that fall, someone tipped off the media about my coaching three sports at three different schools, and an article was written in one of the papers. It somehow became a statewide story, and I started to receive calls from other newspapers wanting to do a story on it. I refused, as I didn't think it was a big deal. I truly was just trying to help people out and share my so-called expertise with kids who needed it. I don't have ulterior motives when it comes to helping people out. My parents have trained me well!

When it came time for the 1997-98 basketball season, excitement and enthusiasm were high. Besides the high number of returnees we had, we also had two freshmen, (one who went on to become an all-time track performer in the state of Iowa) who stepped in immediately to give us a huge boost. It also helped that my three seniors were all editors of the yearbook, so we were able to establish an even better bond because of the work we did together for the yearbook. We jumped out to a 4-0 start and did not have the long losing streaks like the year before. Unfortunately, we had two outstanding teams with Denison (who finished second in 4A that year) and Carroll Kuemper in our conference, and they took it to us four times. However, we completed the regular season at 12-7, and looked forward to tournament play. Because of some scheduling conflicts, we knew our first two tournament games would be in Atlantic, so we thought we had a chance to make it to state.

We played a great first game and defeated Red Oak and good friend Glenn Mason to advance to the regional semi-final at home against rival Kuemper. It was a strange game as we were the "visitor" and they brought a large crowd so it didn't seem like a home game. Our kids played an aggressive game, and we were up by one with two minutes left. However, Kuemper made a couple of impressive plays at the end, and we ended up losing by seven. The kids along with the coaches were heartbroken and Kuemper ended up going on to win the state title. I'm not sure if that made us feel better or worse. However, we again had a great nucleus coming back, and I definitely felt like our returning group would get Atlantic back to the state tournament. My prediction ended up being correct. However, I would end up not being on the bench with the team.

CHAPTER 7

FIND YOUR WAY BACK HOME

Home Is Where the Heart Is

In the spring of 1998, I was hired to be the freshmen baseball coach at Atlantic. I thought this was a way for people to see my loyalty to the school and also allowed me to stay with the game of baseball. It was difficult to not run my own program, but I learned a lot from the other coaches and enjoyed my summer. Although I loved everything about basketball at Atlantic, because of my difficult teaching situation, the response to my coaching at other schools, and the fact I was three hours from my hometown, I began to have some thoughts about whether Atlantic was the long-term place for me. I had been someone who kept up on the latest job openings not because I had ever been purposely trying to leave a place, but if there was something that was a better situation than what I had, it would be foolish to not at least take a look at it.

So that spring, when I looked in the paper on a Sunday in April, I saw an opening at Cherokee for middle school social studies, head girls' basketball, and head volleyball. I had driven through Cherokee hundreds of times as it was the almost halfway point between George and Newell when I would drive back and forth on many weekends. It was a great town, and something immediately drew me to that ad. I called Marlin Lode, the superintendent, and he asked me to apply ASAP.

Soon after applying, I received a call from Cherokee that they wanted me to interview with them soon. With my busy schedule, the only time that worked was a Sunday afternoon/evening. So, after spending a couple days with my parents, I stopped in Cherokee on the way back to Atlantic and interviewed with Principal Larry Weede and Athletic Director Todd Williams. I built an immediate bond with Mr. Weede as he had officiated a number of my volleyball matches at Newell-Fonda and actually remembered coaching Cherokee baseball against me when I played at George. Anyone that has a positive recollection of my athletic career is high in my book!

After meeting with Mr. Weede, I asked to see where I would teach. He basically asked why I would want to do that and said we didn't have to, but I insisted. He finally took me to a big, old, brick building called Wilson Middle School, and I soon found out why he didn't want me to see it! The building had a lot of wear and tear, no air conditioning, and lots of steps. Considering I was working at a brand new high school in Atlantic, the building was a big turn off. I wasn't quite sure how teaching middle school would work as well.

However, talking to Mr. Weede and Mr. Williams built a lot of enthusiasm in me about coming to Cherokee. I knew they would be great people to work for and would be 100% supportive. When I was leaving, they said, "The job is yours." Ok then.... since I went in with no expectations, suddenly coming face to face with this new opportunity was exciting but also scary as to what to do.

I jumped in the car to head the two hours back to Atlantic. The first song I heard on the radio was "Searching My Soul" by Vonda Shepard which was from the Ally McBeal TV show that was popular at the time. A couple of the lyrics hit me hard; "I've been searching my soul tonight. I know there's so much more to life. Now I know I can shine the light to find my way back home."

Interesting...Cherokee would be much closer to home...my parents would be able to watch me coach much more...my teaching and coaching would be better so it definitely got me thinking. The rest of the song's lyrics hit home as well. By the time I had been on the road a half hour, I was certain I wanted to take the position. I had been communicating with Mr. Sweeney and Mr. Herring at the high school about my discussions with Cherokee, and they had been very supportive, but I knew they would be very disappointed, and they were. However, they were very appreciative of the work I had done and wished me well. They were very classy about everything, and I was very thankful.

I knew the toughest part of leaving was yet to come in letting people, especially my team, know that I was leaving them. I knew I needed to do this quickly before word got out, and I wanted the team to hear from me. School was still in session so I asked a good friend and the girls' track coach, Bruce Henderson (who would lead his team to four straight state titles starting in 1998) if I could have the basketball players after school, and of course, he said yes.

When word got out about the meeting, I had a number of players stop and ask, "Why are we meeting?" I just said, "Don't worry; it will be short!" When I walked in, the room got quiet, and I kept it short. The moment I said I was leaving, I heard one of my post players gasp audibly. A couple got tears in their eyes. Most just sat there in stunned silence. I knew I was letting them down, but I also knew their future was bright (they went on to make the state tournament the next two years). I certainly wasn't leaving because of them and tried to communicate that, but I felt I didn't do a very good job.

Telling my assistants, Dick Casady and Kathy Sarasio, as well as my great friend Coach Jenkins that I was leaving was also difficult. I had filled them in about what was happening, but it was still tough. The toughest part of leaving was a feeling of letting people down. I wouldn't have left for any other job but

Cherokee, but I'm sure a lot of people never forgave me for leaving and didn't understand. If I had stayed at Atlantic, I think I would have been very happy but looking back, I know it was the right decision. It was a whirlwind after that trying to get a house sold in Atlantic, a house bought in Cherokee, get moved, and get my coaching started in Cherokee. I was also coaching freshmen baseball in Atlantic that summer so there was little time for rest.

One weekend in June, I had gone home to the folks for a day, and I had then stopped in Cherokee on Sunday for some work with the volleyball and basketball players. When I left George earlier in the day, the weather had said SW Iowa was going to receive a lot of rain shortly, and I began to run into some rain when I left Cherokee. When I got to Denison about half way to Atlantic, I finally got the Atlantic radio station in my car (no cell phones or XM radio back then!) when all I could hear was news about the "large flood" in Atlantic and how people could not get into Atlantic as roads were closed.

I found out later that Atlantic recorded over 13 inches of rain during that 24-hour period, which at the time was the highest amount ever recorded in state history! Uh oh...what is going on with my house, and how will I get home? When I got to my usual entry road into Atlantic, sure enough, it was blocked. The radio said the south entry into town was open so I drove all the way around on the interstate and was finally able to get to my house. When I arrived home, I had a couple of inches of water in my basement and a light fixture on the main floor had water coming through it along with a nice amount on the floor. Fortunately, the overall damage was pretty minimal, and I was able to clean things up pretty quickly. However, it did seem to be another sign that it was time for me to move on.

I spent some time in Cherokee looking at houses and could never seem to find just the right house for me. I had spent some time staying with my new AD Todd Williams at his beautiful, split-level house in north Cherokee. He was going through a divorce and was going to move into another house but had not put his house on the market yet. One day he said, "Why don't you just buy my house?" It was MUCH bigger than I needed and more money than I had planned to spend. However, it had a huge backyard with an attached garage and was a great house. After a lot of thought, I finally decided to buy it, which took a big load off my mind. Unfortunately, my Atlantic house did not sell right away, but fortunately a buyer was found early fall.

When moving day arrived, I decided to rent a large U-Haul to move everything. The folks came down to help and a good number of friends including Coach Maske and my Atlantic coaching friends came over to help as well. I remember we all tried to figure out how to move the hot tub. We had at least eight men with at least a couple who were very strong, and we expected the task to be an easy one. We all took an end and on the count of three tried to lift it but nothing moved. I remember Coach Maske saying, "Did your end move? Mine didn't." Another friend said, "Did you drain the water first?" Yes I did! After a lot of thought, we found some carts and after tilting the hot tub on a side, we got it wheeled to the truck and then finally loaded. When we got to Cherokee, another large crew including Todd Williams and Larry Weede helped us unload the truck. We had another difficult time with the hot tub, it had to sit in the garage for a while, but we got everything unloaded. It was time to get to the tasks at hand and get ready for a new job as a teacher and a coach.

The crew trying to move the hot tub!

The summer of 1998 came, and I was knee deep in camps and open gyms since I coached both volleyball and basketball. The players were very receptive to everything I wanted to do in both sports, and I was excited to get started. Parents were great supporters of the events, and we had impressive numbers in both programs.

When the volleyball season started, I knew we might struggle a bit going in, but I expected us to be pretty competitive. Unfortunately, as the season started, it was clear we weren't going to win much. Back then, you could have ties in volleyball so we did have a few of those, but unfortunately, as the season wound down, we had no wins. I noticed my "intensity" and anger level rising as the season went on. It seemed like I yelled so much and put too much pressure on the team to win. Kids were working hard, but I think I was so embarrassed by the losing that it affected my coaching. Thankfully, I didn't check my blood pressure as I probably would have been put on medication!

We got to the last regular season tournament of the year at Storm Lake with no wins but with hope of success as we were playing two teams we had played earlier and had given them a battle. In these tournaments, the team played two games instead of two out of three, so if the games were split, it went down as a tie. When we would win the first game, there was huge pressure to win game two as that was the only way to get a win. Unfortunately, I knew that better than anyone and undoubtedly put a ton of pressure on the team to win those games.

Our first match of the day was against Spirit Lake. We won a close first game and held the lead in game two. I don't exactly remember the last couple of plays, but we pulled out the second game and therefore our first match of the year. It was like we won the state title! Someone took a picture of our fans (my parents were there), and they all had a huge celebration! We went on to win another match that day against Sioux City North, but then lost later in the week in the first round of regional tournaments to Maurice-Orange City-Floyd Valley so we ended up with two wins for the season.

Mom and Dad at a Cherokee volleyball match

During my nine years at Cherokee, our volleyball program made huge strides. We had winning records the last four years including a 26-11 mark overall and 7-1 in the conference. We never won a conference title or made it to state, but that was mostly because of having to play Hull Western Christian, Unity Christian, or MOC-FV every year. They were high school volleyball powerhouses, and we never had quite enough to defeat them.

It was usually frustrating playing Western Christian as they were so good and so talented, tall and athletic and most of the time, our teams were intimidated when we played them, so even being competitive was difficult. Hull was only about 10 miles from where I grew up so I knew the school well. WC had an arrogance about them and that supreme confidence rubbed a lot of people the wrong way. Obviously, they were very good and that high confidence level made them even better.

One memory of that time was when we played them in a regional match in Hull. We were decent, but they were ranked #1 or #2 in the state so we knew it was almost impossible to pull out a win. The only fans we had were a few parents including mine, and we had zero students at the match while Western Christian had a large student section.

We lost game one by a large number and were totally intimidated. When the game was over, their student section got up, ran around the court once, and proceeded to sit directly behind our bench. During timeouts, they would yell and scream and be as loud as they could making it almost impossible to be heard. This continued the rest of the match. I happened to look over at the WC coach and principal, and they both were laughing and were very amused by the whole thing.

At no point did I say anything to them about what was happening. Now, I'm sure you are wondering why I didn't complain to someone about the behavior? One, I think **players and teams need to be able to handle all sorts of challenges and need to be able to respond and do their job. This is a life skill. If someone is always solving their problems for them, players will never learn how to do things right on their own.**

Secondly, I guess I did expect someone from Western Christian (especially being a Christian school) to step up and take responsibility for what was going on. Obviously, they were the better team, but clearly they were rubbing it in. Unfortunately, the student behavior continued the rest of the match and not surprisingly, the match ended very quickly.

The next day, a Cherokee fan wrote a letter to the principal at Western Christian to talk about the incident and asked what he thought of it. The principal called back and said it was a good match with good crowd support. When the fan asked about the student section, he mentioned that they were a nice group and supported the team well. The fan then proceeded to say she was very ashamed to admit to the people of Cherokee that she was a member of the Reformed Church at George, especially since Western Christian was with the Reformed faith and her church did NOT believe in how the students and principal made fun of another school. She said her church would not do what that student section did.

The principal immediately backtracked, apologized, and said he would call me, which he did. I thanked him for calling and took the high road, saying he had a great team, but that I would never allow our student section to do what they did (the Western coach got in on the fun as well. He promised he would meet with the student body to discuss their actions and that was the end of that. Oh, by the way, who was the caller? It was my mom!

As I think back to my volleyball coaching days, I think of a lot of hot gyms, a lot of long Saturdays, a lot of struggles but also a lot of fun. I wish I had been more patient with players as I definitely think I put too much pressure on them and with the time in between points, it undoubtedly didn't help a lot of players to perform better. Most of my players also played basketball so real bonds were built, and it was great to be able to set up open gym and weightlifting times without worrying about conflicts. Some people asked about the difficulties of coaching back to back seasons, but I had always done that, and I wasn't married at the time so I never had an issue with it.

My basketball teams at Cherokee started slowly like volleyball did. The previous coach, Steve Blair, had mentioned that there was a good sophomore group coming up although they were not very tall. How true that was! There were a lot of 5'4" kids and not much height, but they were a scrappy group, and I knew the running and pressing style I wanted to utilize would work pretty well with them.

My first game at Cherokee was a memorable one as we played Spencer who would turn into a big rival during the years. We unveiled our run, press, and shoot three's type of play that would carry us through the time at Cherokee. Unfortunately, I remember really cold shooting, and a lot of turnovers in that first game but also a lot of hustle and grit. We ended up winning 49-46!

Unfortunately, that was one of the few wins that year. One of the tougher losses was when my hometown Little Rock Mustangs from George came to town and beat us by 12. The coach, Ken Roseberry, had been one of my PE teachers and was a hall of fame coach. Ken was another old-school coach, and I admired the type of team he put together. We were the bigger school and should have won the game but cold shooting did us in.

The first season was a good one with a lot of hard work and enthusiasm, but we managed to only win six games. With an experienced group coming back, expectations were high going into the 1999-2000 season. Early in the year, we traveled to George to play my alma mater in what could best be described as a strange game. To coach in the same gym that you played in was a great honor but was very surreal. The players didn't quite understand when we drove up and I joked, "I wonder what they did with the statue of me that was up from my playing days?" We all know that was not the truth! I think our players knew how badly I wanted to win that game, and we came through 54-42. To win in that gym with so many family and friends there will certainly go down as a career highlight. It made me realize that leaving Atlantic for Cherokee was the right thing to do. I'm not sure what happened, but maybe we were concerned about the upcoming Y2K and the start of the new century issues. We did not play well going to the holiday break and my coaches and I struggled to turn things around. We were 4-7 and knew that we should be a lot better than that.

At the time, the Lakes Conference had nine teams so we came up with the idea of winning the "mythical" second half of the conference title. We said we were starting over, and our record was 0-0. We told the team if we won the second half, we would get them medals and make a big deal of it. For whatever reason, we turned it around during that second half of the season and went 8-3 with two of those losses in overtime. We went 7-1 in that second half of the conference, losing only to dreaded Western Christian in overtime.

The last regular season game was at home against Spencer and was our senior night. The only thing I could think of was, "This is for the conference title, and we have to win." We had three seniors that year, one who started and two that came off the bench. In the past senior nights, I had tried to either start the seniors or make sure they played. Because we had been playing well, I decided to keep the same starting line up and do everything we could to win. The game was a tough battle as it always was with Spencer, and we were down eight going into the fourth quarter. However, we hit some clutch three's and free throws, and in a very exciting environment, we won the game by four. The team was thrilled after the game. Everyone was ecstatic, and we were so proud of what we had done! It was one of the best moments of my coaching career to that point!

After the game, I went to the lobby to visit with some people when a dad of one of the seniors confronted me and literally backed me against the wall. He used a number of choice words that I would rather not repeat here. I tried to explain to him why I did what I did and that the team including his daughter was thrilled with the win, and she showed no negative emotions. I was doing what was best for the team. That didn't help, and he continued to crowd me at the wall, but I kept my cool surprisingly well. Finally, an administrator stepped in and got the parent out of there. It was one of the few times in my career I felt physically threatened.

After the incident, I went back to the player and apologized to her for not playing. She was fine and said it wasn't a problem, but I wasn't sure if she was covering for her dad or whether she truly was OK. The incident took away from the win, but it definitely made me think about how I handled senior night activities going forward. As a head coach, I have to be thinking about what is best for the team. However, what role does thinking about the big picture of what your program stands for play in this? Is there a way to honor seniors who have meant so much to your program without sacrificing the big goal of winning the game?

The answer and what I have done since that night is to start my seniors on senior night, and if we have a number of seniors, the ones who never start get that opportunity. That doesn't mean I play them the whole game but being introduced and then being in at the beginning is a huge honor to the player and the family. They have been a tremendous part of our program for four years, and they have earned the right to be honored in this way! If we lose a game because of these early minutes of the game, then we didn't deserve to win anyway!

This incident with the senior parent was one of the worst I have ever experienced as a coach, and I hope I never experience something like that again. It left a lasting impression on me. However, it turned into one of the best learning experiences of my career and showed that **we all learn from life events, even ones that are definitely negative. We can't be so set in our ways that we aren't willing to listen and learn throughout our lives.**

CHAPTER 8

EVERYONE WE MEET IMPACTS OUR LIVES
Everyone We Meet Has a Story to Tell

Before I talk further about my time at Cherokee, I need to share some memories about four of the more unique people I met at Cherokee. The first was Steve Blair. Steve is probably one of the most honest and upfront people I have ever met. If you looked up the picture of an "old school" coach somewhere, you would probably find Coach Blair's picture. I had run into him a number of times when our Newell-Fonda teams scrimmaged Cherokee and thought his teams were tough, physical, and big (one of his former players was 6'4" Tammi Blackstone who went on to star at Drake). I also remembered his teams always wore kneepads, and he always wore pants.

In our first conversation, Steve let me know that the reason he quit was because of parent issues. He no longer could handle it and wanted to pass the reigns on to someone else. He could have been bitter that I was taking his place, but instead he was amazingly helpful and was someone I could talk to. Within a couple of years of my time at Cherokee, he offered to coach middle school girls' basketball. What a blessing to have a coach like that working on fundamentals at the middle school to feed into my high school coaching program. It was no surprise that our state appearances started when the kids we worked with in middle school reached the high school level.

One piece of advice Coach Blair gave me was with regards to his manager, Natasha Olhausen, or "Nana" as everyone knew her. Nana had Down's Syndrome but never let it define her. Steve mentioned that Nana had graduated a few years earlier but continued to volunteer as a manager. His comment was, "She will do anything you want her to do, but she will drive you crazy!" How true that ended up to be!

When I first met Nana during the summer of 1998, it was clear how passionate she was about the Braves. I discovered quickly that I probably didn't want her to keep stats as she constantly forgot to keep track of things because she was yelling "REBOUND" or "Go Braves!" However, she loved to fill water bottles so we found some other people to do stats and kept her duties simple. Since I coached volleyball and basketball, Nana willingly signed up for both duties.

Over the next nine years, there are so many stories to tell about this amazing person! She loved our bus trips and many times sat right behind the coaches and me. Not that I didn't enjoy visiting with her, but she literally never stopped talking! At times I would have to tell her, "Nana, the older girls want to talk to you in the back" just to keep my sanity. She would ask, "Which one," and I always said, "I think all of them!" The players were so good to her and made her feel right at home, which I greatly appreciated.

Eventually, she was becoming more of a distraction than a help so I sat down with her one day and told her I wanted her to stop managing and become a super fan so she could sit in the stands and yell as much as she wanted. Nana definitely was opposed to this at first but eventually thought about it and said, "I can still come to games, right?" I told her, "Of course you can!"

Nana got a job at Hy-Vee and every time I would see her there, she would literally come running over and say, "Coach, how are we going to be this year? Are we going to make it to state?" I always said, "We are getting better, and we'll make it eventually." Whenever she saw my parents at games, she had to go over and say, "Hi coach's mom and dad!" Nana still found a way to make it to a lot of games as Duane and Marcia Henke and Steve and Jean Benson let her ride with them.

When we finally made it to state in 2003 for the first time, Nana called me a number of times during the week with questions before the game and told me that she was so excited she couldn't sleep! It seemed like she always had a Cherokee Braves shirt on and supported all activities. Eventually the school gave her a lifetime pass to attend all Braves games for free, which was a well-deserved honor.

Later on when we left Cherokee, I knew that Nana had been experiencing some health issues but it still came as a big shock when I received word that she had passed away suddenly in November of 2014. The outpouring of support from the community was amazing and the local TV stations even did reports on her. Unfortunately because of basketball (ironically!), we were not able to make it back for the funeral, but I'm sure she understood. What an amazing life Nana led. She never let her Down's Syndrome and other issues keep her down. She was always positive and clearly made an impact on everyone she met. I was impressed with how the whole Cherokee community treated her and made her feel welcome. The world needs more of that!

Another of the unique people I first met at Cherokee was Larry Weede, who was my principal at Cherokee Middle School. Obviously, his last name gives you a chuckle, but I soon discovered what an amazing man he was. I had met him previously, as he was a well-known volleyball official so I had run into him many times at Newell-Fonda. It made me glad I tried to be nice to officials. As I mentioned earlier, he also claimed that he remembered coaching against me in baseball when he was Cherokee's coach, and he thought I was a very good player. I did question his memory at that point!

Mr. Weede was an amazing principal to work with in the school setting. People ALWAYS came first with him. It didn't matter if you were a staff or student, he had time for people. One thing that impressed me from the beginning was that he told the newest students who were fifth graders at CMS that if he didn't know their first name after a month of school, he would buy them ice cream. Also, when staff members had their retirement parties, he wrote original poems totally dedicated to that staff member. There are not many principals who would do such a thoughtful thing!

Mr. Weede's educational philosophy could be summed up this way in my opinion. It was to hire good people and get out of their way! Encourage them and be there when they need you but don't micromanage their jobs. I know he rarely came into my classroom, and I told him he was welcome to come in any time. He would say, "I know, but I don't want to bother you. I talk to kids, and I know you are doing a great job." Mr. Weede's door was open if I had questions and when a parent questioned something a teacher was doing at school, we all knew he would be there to support us.

Mr. Weede may not have been an expert on every educational issue out there, but he knew how to put faith in people. I have tried to be that way with people, especially my assistants. **If you believe in people, give them responsibilities, give them support, and then let them go to work, you will usually find more success.**

A final person I met right away at Cherokee who had a huge impact on my career was Leo Hupke, PE teacher and coach of literally every sport you can imagine. He was one of my basketball assistants at Cherokee but also helped with football, track, and softball. Coach Hupke could also be labeled as "old school," and no one worked as hard as he did for athletes. Like Coach Blair, Leo was a straight shooter, and I could go to him for great advice. It didn't hurt that his wife Kathy was an amazing cook and since I was single at the time, I was often invited to the Hupkes for a meal. Their door was always open.

Coach Hupke loved having breakfast at Hy-Vee on Saturday mornings. Many times I would try to sleep in a bit on Saturday's when about 8:30 my phone would ring. "This is pain in the a _ _ Hupke. What are you doing?" he would ask. "Just reading the paper," I would reply. "What are you doing?" He replied, "I'm in your driveway; do you want to go to breakfast?" I'd look out my window and there he was in his old truck. Of course, I would scramble to get dressed and head out with him. Those were great times, and we would rehash the previous night's game, activities that were happening at school, or any other world problems we could solve. I picked his brain on numerous topics, and I wish younger coaches and teachers today would do that more often. I think sometimes people are embarrassed to ask for help or feel their questions aren't appropriate. **We should all be trying to learn from others, no matter what their age.**

One thing I noticed Leo doing often that I thought was impressive was that he would call random people from his past that he hadn't talked to for a while just to see how they were doing. It might be someone who had previous health issues, someone who had lost a loved one, or just someone he hadn't talked to for a while. When I moved to Mason City, I would get a random call from him as well. How meaningful just a few minutes of time on the phone are to people who might need some encouragement.

Later on in my time at Cherokee, I helped Leo coach softball when he could not find an assistant for the summer. Softball coaches didn't have to dress like players as baseball coaches do, but we did have to wear Cherokee shirts. I noticed that often Coach Hupke wore a shirt that said CQI on it. I finally asked him what that meant. He said, "Continuous Quality Improvement." I loved that and how true it is for the classroom and for athletic endeavors! **You should always be working on something, it should be quality, and it should be getting better!** Now, when I asked him if umpires ever asked how this shirt relates to Cherokee, he said it then became "Cherokee Quality Improvement." It still worked and showed his sense of humor as well.

Coach Hupke had the best interests of students and athletes at heart. I found that there was not a selfish bone in his body. It was NEVER about him but about his athletes and making sure they had a great experience. He also did a great job of supporting all activities at Cherokee, not just those he was involved in. Coach Hupke pushed athletes to be in multiple sports and also supported them in music, the arts, and other activities. He knew well-rounded young people would have the best chance of success down the road. I believe his greatest joy was watching those young people grow and change for the better, which is why he coached so many different sporting events. The world would be a much better place if we had more people like Leo J. Hupke!

CHAPTER 9

NEW BEGINNINGS IN A DIFFERENT WAY

It's Never Too Late to Make a Change

You may have noticed that to this point, there has not been a mention of a wife or any other sort of relationship. That is basically because there was not much information to share, other than I'm sure most women didn't want to put up with me. As I mentioned earlier, despite Mom's best efforts, I made it to my 35th birthday in 2000 as a single man, and it never really bothered me. Of course, I had thought about being married and having kids, but I had never met the right person and wasn't going to jump into a wrong relationship.

I think my general shyness growing up probably held me back some and although I had a bunch of girls who were friends, I had very few girlfriends over time. There were a few relationships that started but never really materialized into anything. The shyness was a huge issue in high school and college along with general disinterest in dating. During my time at Newell, there were very few single women my age, and the Internet was just starting so dating sites and other options weren't available. At Cherokee, I started to date a bit more and had a promising relationship in the winter of 2000, but because of too much pushing the relationship on my part, we grew apart and it ended. Although it had lasted more than a month, I had not said anything to my family as I did not want them to get their hopes up too high which turned out to be a good move on my part.

One day late that summer, I was having a conversation about this with a friend of mine at school. He said, "Have you ever checked out some of those dating websites? You should check those out. I know people who have tried them and had some success." I actually laughed out loud when I first heard him say that. Who does stuff like that? I thought he was joking! He was convinced it was worth trying so I decided to give it a try myself. What did I have to lose? I signed up for one of the dating sites and started checking it out.

One of the first listings I saw was for a pretty blonde from North Central Iowa, and we had a number of things in common. I decided to send her a message and surprisingly, she responded fairly quickly. I found out her name was Margaret (my grandmother's name was Margaret!), but her friends called her Margo, and she lived in Belmond, Iowa, about an hour and 45 minutes from Cherokee. She had grown up in Mason City, was an only child, and worked as a graphic artist. She was a Macintosh expert and was amazingly smart about anything related to technology. We continued to message for a stretch of time before I finally asked for her number. We proceeded to call and talk a few times, and the conversations were great.

I finally asked one day in September if we could meet, and I offered to drive to Belmond. I remember vividly parking in the lot of her apartment where she lived above a catering business and being scared to death about how it would go. We ended up going to Cattlemen's Steak House and had a great meal, even though I spilled pop all over the table at one point! We both had a good laugh about that and generally had a good time. However, when I left that night to drive back home, I wasn't sure if things would continue as Margo seemed pretty reserved about

*The first day Margo came to my folks'
and saw their dog buddy*

everything, and I, of course, assumed she wasn't really that interested in me. Fortunately, a couple days later, I had a note back from her and figured out that she was hoping to continue a relationship.

We started dating and switched off weekends with who drove to see whom. One of our first big dates was a Matchbox Twenty Concert in Ames where I'm sure she figured out quickly that I am not musically inclined! I broke down and told my family about Margo, and they were thrilled! When I finally took her back to George to meet everyone, she was concerned that my family would like her. HA! They loved her!

Our first event together at Cherokee was a home football game. I tried to warn Margo ahead of time that she would be bombarded with questions and attacked by middle school students. I was right as kids came flocking over to us despite our best efforts to stay as far back as possible. I was impressed that she didn't turn and leave town at that point! When it came to meeting her parents, Margo was again worried. "They aren't going to like you. They haven't liked any of my boyfriends." HA! I wasn't worried because I had great confidence that I could relate to them. Fortunately, we hit it off right away. More than 15 years later, I still get along great with her parents, and they are some of my biggest supporters.

My relationship with Margo continued to grow, and I specifically remember spending a Sunday at her apartment February 18, 2001. She was busy doing a few things so I sat down to watch the end of the Daytona 500. There was a large crash at the end of the race, and it was oddly quiet at the end of the telecast. As I drove home that night, I found out that Dale Earnhardt, legendary NASCAR driver, had died in the crash. As a racecar fan, that was a devastating blow and the outpouring of emotion from so many people was amazing.

The only problem with our relationship was the distance between us. Since basketball season was going on, Margo did most of the driving on weekends and most people know how "wonderful" the roads in North Iowa can get in the winter! She had a number of harrowing trips, and I hated having her on the road.

One day in February, I noticed our local newspaper had an ad in it for a graphic artist, which was her exact area of expertise. We talked it over and decided that she should apply. If she got the position, she would move to Cherokee. I remember calling Mom and telling her the plan. In typical Mom fashion, she said, "Oh...you are going to live together...don't you think if you are taking that big a step that you should get married? However, do what you have to do." Honestly, I had been thinking some of those same thoughts. However, we had only been dating for five months so was it the right thing, would she say yes, how would it work, etc?

I finally decided to propose and the question was where and when? We had decided to go to the state basketball tournament the first week of March so I figured that was as good a time as any. I headed to Belmond to pick Margo up, we went to games in Des Moines, and then I told her I was going back to Des Moines. Little did she know that I stayed in Belmond, went to her apartment, set some clues up around her place, and then waited for her to return. When Margo returned, she found the clues and me hiding. Fortunately, she said YES!

We drove to Mason City to see her parents. Her mom worked at NIACC and was thrilled when we stopped there. Her dad was working at a car dealership.

He was behind a desk when we stopped. When Margo showed him the ring, it took him a minute to figure out what was going on before he finally stood and shook Margo's hand! We give him a hard time about that even today. He claimed he was so shocked he didn't know how to respond!

The next step was planning the wedding and trying to figure out where and when it would be. Margo got the job at the paper and moved to Cherokee so we decided since her family was small and most of the people coming to the wedding were close to Cherokee, we would have it there. Neither of us had a home church that we attended regularly, but I had gone to the Lutheran church down the street and knew the minister well so we decided to have him perform the ceremony.

We struggled to find a place for the ceremony. One day as I arrived to teach at the middle school, a thought came to me. My classroom had moved from the old, brick building I started at to a beautiful new building close to our house. The building had a very nice commons area with a skylight and would have enough room for a gathering. What if we had the wedding there? It was a crazy idea, but when I went home and asked Margo about it, she was fine with it, and we decided to ask permission from Mr. Weede and the school. They were very supportive and told us to go for it! We settled on July 28th as the date as we had to schedule around camps, the start of volleyball, and the start of the school year. Fortunately, my bride was the opposite of a "bridezilla" and decisions were made quickly. We decided on no singing and instead asked the high school orchestra to perform since I knew all of the students in that group. They performed beautifully!

The wedding went off without a hitch. It was VERY hot, and about a half hour before the ceremony as guests were starting to arrive, my nephew Kevin (one of the ushers) came back to where I was and said, "Uncle Curt, the commons is getting very hot and people are starting to complain about the heat." I knew there was an override button in the commons for the air conditioning to kick back in, so I went out, said hello to everyone, pushed the button, and got everything cooled off!

A memorable moment after the wedding was being driven around town in a convertible by our great friend and next-door neighbor, Ken Lee. Ken and his wife Molly were the nicest people alive, and whenever I needed help with anything, I knew they were there. They were so selfless and always took time to help when needed. I think he enjoyed driving around that day as much as we did!

More than 15 years later, Margo and I are still going strong. Not every day has been great and many obstacles have had to be overcome. However, I feel so blessed to have found her, and it's not a coincidence that my biggest coaching

Leaving the wedding with our neighbor Ken Lee

achievements have come since we were married. Margo is not a big sports fan so after games, we spend zero time rehashing things and just move on with life. Before marriage, I would stay up until all hours, dissecting tape, second questioning how the game had gone, and basically living and dying with every game.

My wife has brought perspective to my life, which is something I desperately needed. No longer are games and practices life and death to me. She has broadened my horizons in so many ways and keeps me humble at all times. She lets me do what I love and supports me unconditionally with that. Margo hates having any attention drawn to her and would rather stay out of the spotlight, but I wouldn't be able to do what I do without her.

Our first couple of months of marriage provided some challenges. I was teaching seventh grade social studies and coaching volleyball at Cherokee at the time, and Margo had just taken a job as the technology coordinator at the school and got really sick on the 10th of September in 2001. She ended up staying home much of that week so I spent a lot of time trying to be a caregiver.

I was teaching in my room on September 11th when one of our special education teachers came in and said, "You need to turn your TV on!" When we turned it on, we saw that a plane had hit one of the World Trade Center Towers. We decided to leave the TV on and watch it develop. As we were watching, the second plane hit another tower. It's hard to describe the reaction. I knew right then this was more than just an accident. We did debate that day whether to keep the coverage on or not. Were seventh graders able to deal properly with such a tragedy? We decided to watch, discuss, and try to alleviate their fears and concerns. I believe it was the right decision and our principal concurred, but you definitely wonder when working with students at that age.

However, my memories of 9-11 will always be connected with another tragedy that happened at the end of that day. One of our eighth grade students and a former student of mine was killed late at night in an accident where he was riding with his brother who survived. I remember walking into school on the 12th and being told there was an emergency staff meeting. I assumed we were getting info on 9-11, but instead, we were told the student had passed away, and we had to plan the day and how to let the students know.

Talking to kids about this was one of the hardest things I've had to do as a teacher. CMS is a fairly small middle school so most students knew Kyle, but we had various responses from deep grief, indifference, and silence so basically, what you would expect from middle schoolers. Our staff did an amazing job that week but with the double tragedies, there was very little academic learning going on. However, it was definitely a life lesson on dealing with tragedy, communicating your thoughts, being there for others, and continuing to live your life.

Another aspect of the week was coaching volleyball. Many of my players knew Kyle or were classmates of his brother, so they were deeply affected. We had our annual Saturday tournament that weekend and because of everything going on, we debated canceling the event. We decided to play and felt that keeping some normalcy in the lives of our players was the best way to go. I ended up coaching our first match in a suit and tie, went to Kyle's funeral, and then came back to coach the rest of the day. I have no idea what we did that day as that whole week is pretty much a blur and something I never want to go through again.

Looking back, I'm not sure how we made it through that week with everything that happened. If there are personal lessons I took from that week, it would be **the importance of being there for people, communicating feelings to others, being aware of what is going on around you, and continuing to live while going through tragedies and keeping as much normalcy in your life as possible during those times. Unfortunately, life is sometimes about being dealt tough body blows that knock us down to our core. It is our life's job though to keep living and honor the memories of those we have lost. Never forget!**

CHAPTER 10

NOBODY SAID IT WOULD BE EASY

Nothing in Life Is Ever Easy

Getting back to basketball action, we went into the 2000-2001 season with high expectations as we had six seniors who had played a lot and played well together. One of the best wins of that season was going to Newell-Fonda and beating my great friend Coach Maske and his Mustangs 55-39. We did it by playing NF basketball while running, pressing, and making 11 three's! This was the third season we had played them, and they had pummeled us the previous two years. It was especially gratifying to beat them in Newell where I had spent so much time and had so much respect for all of the people there. I wouldn't be half the coach or person I am today without the help of Coach Maske and all of the great people at Newell-Fonda.

Again playing a tough schedule, we managed to go 13-9 and again lost in tournaments to Maurice-Orange City-Floyd Valley. It was a bitter defeat as that group had played together for so long and had put so much time and effort into the game. For whatever reason, we could never get over the hump with that group. Other teams were just a bit taller and more athletic, but none had more heart than our group did.

Going into the 2001-02 season, I expected us to drop a bit as the six seniors we lost had garnered most of the playing time, and we would be inexperienced. We did have a great group of freshmen, and I figured they would probably be part of the mix. A couple of them had been managers of the high school team when they were in middle school so they knew what to expect coming in.

The season started slowly, and it was downhill from there. We had trouble scoring, we had trouble breaking a press, and we had trouble understanding why three freshmen were playing. You name it, we had trouble with it. The kids played hard but again, but with the competition we were playing, that wasn't good enough. I took quite a bit of heat that year for playing three freshmen, two who started most of the year. We had a number of older players, but they had not put in the time the younger players had, plus I knew the freshmen would only get better. Those three had played some with the older girls in years past when we couldn't get enough kids to go to camp so I knew they would keep working. I have always been of the philosophy that **you play the best players, period. The coaches make that decision, and you move forward.** Age doesn't have anything to do with it.

If you need a doctor, do you want the oldest, or the best? If you need a good lawyer, do you want the oldest or the best? You get my point, hopefully. **Great high school and college teams play their best kids no matter what their age. If you don't do that, what incentive is there for players to work and get better?** Without this philosophy, players will just wait their turn and know they will play when they are older. Over the years, I have been told occasionally that I favor players. I am guilty as charged. **I will always favor players who work hard, have a great attitude, and buy into the team concept. I could care less what grade a player is in, who their parents are, how much money their parents have.**

Honestly, I am selfish in the fact that I want to put the best team possible on the floor because that makes me look the best. Why would I purposely play someone who is not going to help us win over someone else who would make the team better? No coach does that. One of our responsibilities as teachers and coaches is to teach life lessons and help individuals grow and understand a bit of what the real world is about. **Having high expectations and making sure athletes know they have to earn what they get is a great lesson for everyone no matter what age!**

Back to the 2001-2002 season: we finished 4-18 and probably broke some unknown school records for fewest points, most turnovers, and other unknown lows. Add on to that a very poor coaching job on my part, and it resulted in a bad record. By the end of the season, I knew a number of parents were upset with my performance, and I began to wonder 1) if I was going to be fired at some point and 2) how long I wanted to keep coaching? However, we were only going to lose one senior so with everyone coming back, it had to get better, right?

CHAPTER 11

SEASONS TO REMEMBER

With Great Sorrow Can Come Great Joy

The summer of 2002 continued a string of bad news from my end. One day, we got a call from Mom, who said, "We took your dad to the doctor and they ran tests; he has a tumor in his bladder." That pretty much knocks the breath out of you. Dad was 73 at the time but had been in good health. It was probably a miracle that his cancer was found. He had been mowing the lawn with a riding mower and the ground was quite bumpy. He came in one day and had blood in his urine. If you knew my dad, he was a quiet sort and kept things to himself. He also was not a complainer. For some reason, he told Mom about the blood. Thank you, Dad! She immediately called the doctor, and luckily, they could get him in. Fortunately, the specialist happened to be there and requested that they do more tests immediately.

Those tests showed a tumor at the end of his bladder and in a bad spot to try and get to for any kind of treatment. More tests showed the cancer had not spread, which was a huge blessing. However, the doctor wanted to start on some sort of treatment as soon as possible so that it would not spread. Fortunately, he did not need full chemotherapy at that point and they began with what was called chemo washes where they would go in and "spray" chemo directly on the tumor to see if it would shrink at all. Chemo washes and scrapings inside the bladder didn't help as the tumor kept growing, but the tumor had NOT grown through the walls of the bladder so that was why it was contained. So Dad needed no chemo treatments and stayed cancer free in the rest of his body.

This continued off and on for a number of months that fall. Unfortunately, the washes were proven to not be effective and the decision was made that he would need surgery. Doctors would remove his bladder and prostate as well since it was so close to the bladder. This would mean he would have a bag for his urine for the rest of his life. The family and I really questioned how he would handle this tremendous lifestyle change, but Mom promised to help him through and kept him positive throughout.

Surgery was set for late December of 2002 in Sioux Falls, and the day came with a lot of dread. The doctors were very upfront about the prospects and told us how serious and how long the surgery was. There were certainly no guarantees and any surgery with someone his age was a concern. All of the family gathered to support Dad. Fortunately, he made it through the surgery with flying colors and doctors were confident they had gotten the tumor and nothing else was there. We knew it was going to be a long recovery, but there was a lot of hope. Unfortunately, there was a major setback to come.

Meanwhile, when the next basketball season was going to start in the fall, and we had signups, things had changed drastically. Coach Hupke had been my assistant for the first four years, and he retired from teaching and coaching. Unfortunately, we had a large number of upperclassmen, including many who had contributed during the last year, decide to not come out. Almost all of our height left the program, and our overall numbers were the lowest I had ever had in a program.

It appeared to the public that things were going to continue to go down hill. However, we had an excellent sophomore class that had gained lots of experience. We had a freshmen class that was talented, and I knew at least one of them was going to come in and play a lot as she had already played varsity softball and volleyball and was an outstanding athlete. We still had three seniors who stuck with it and had gained experience over time. Also that spring, our high school principal had resigned and during the summer, rumors had come in that the replacement had a tall freshmen daughter who was very athletic and had started in softball as an eighth grader. Those rumors were true! Since then, I've always requested that when our school has an administrative opening, one of the prerequisites is that they need to have a tall, athletic daughter! Once I saw her play in the summer, I knew she would be a part of our varsity team.

Practice started, and I had a feeling we weren't going to go 4-18 again. The athletes who returned had gained great confidence, and the freshmen fit right in with what we wanted to do. We started the season with a great win at Pocahontas, and the super start continued. We went to Hull and beat Western Christian for the first time in forever which gave the team loads of confidence.

Before the Christmas break, we beat a good Le Mars team on the road and went into the holiday at 8-0. Our crowd support was off the charts and everyone was amazed with our success. We had a huge student section, and the whole community was getting excited and attending games. Our first two games after break, we continued the winning with victories over Spencer and Spirit Lake to extend our record to 10-0. Suddenly, we were thinking, could we win conference, could we go unbeaten? We were starting to see how good we were!

After the Spirit Lake game, Margo and I went to visit Dad who was still in the hospital in Sioux Falls. It was clear that something wasn't quite right. His color wasn't good, he didn't have much energy, and he looked very defeated. Mom was very aware also and had been bugging the doctor and nurses that something wasn't right. They had run a number of tests and were unable to find anything. We went back home on Sunday unclear of what we were facing.

The next Tuesday, we were to play Battle Creek-Ida Grove on the road in a big game as they were also having a great record and had a freshman who eventually went on to play at Iowa State. We had a lot of pressure on us to keep the unbeaten streak going, and we knew it would not be easy.

The morning of the game, I was at the middle school teaching when I got a call from the office that Mom was on the line. I knew this couldn't be good. She said they had found a leak in Dad's intestine, he was very sick, and they were going to take him into emergency surgery. I told her we would be there as soon as we could. I let the office know that I had to leave, and Mr. Weede covered my classes.

I raced over to the high school as I knew I was going to miss the game. Margo had just taken a job as technology coordinator for the Cherokee Schools so I got to her office and told her we were leaving shortly. Fortunately, my two assistants, Kylee Boettcher and Steve Blair who had taken the freshmen job that year taught at the high school. When I stopped in Kylee's room (a first year teacher and coach and a FANTASTIC ASSISTANT!), she seemed quite nervous, and I assured her that she'd do fine, and just do what we do. Steve had not planned to go to the game but immediately said, "I'll go along, Kylee will coach, and we'll be fine." Not once did I consider staying. I knew the kids were in good hands. Kylee was new but a former college player with great knowledge and great rapport with the kids so I knew she would do a tremendous job. I felt even better with Coach Blair there as his experiences would be vital.

Margo and I jumped in the car and drove a bit (OK, a lot!) over the speed limit to get to Sioux Falls. I remember a few arguments along the way like "SLOW DOWN; it won't do us any good to speed if we die before we get there." I may have slowed down a bit, but the drive seemed to take forever. All I could think of that was Dad was dying, and I wanted us to get there before he went into surgery. We got to the hospital, and the rest of the family was just leaving the room. Mom said they were about to take him to surgery so we made it just in time. We walked in and he smiled and said, "It's about time you got here!" Dad always had a way with words in the hospital and found a way to lighten the mood for those around him! He finally said, "Don't worry, I'll be fine, and I'll see you when it's over." With that, they wheeled him away. I still was worried about the surgery, but I felt so much better after seeing him ahead of time. I knew he was in a good place no matter what happened, and I was content with that.

As we sat in a waiting room for his surgery to end, we tried to make time go faster and unfortunately, someone in our group was very nervous about the outcome of the game, kept asking questions, and saying, "Should we call the radio station or someone to get a score?" This was before radio stations started streaming games so there wasn't a good way to keep track. No, the nervous person wasn't me; it was Mom; I was very calm the whole time and knew the team would be fine. I also knew Dad was in good hands.

The doctors came out after a very long surgery and said that Dad had a long way to go, but he was doing well and should make a complete recovery. Praise God! At that point, Mom broke down and cried. She had been so strong but obviously, she had been under a lot of stress and had been doing what she always did which was to worry about everyone else.

Her next statement was, "We have to find out who won the game!" I finally made a call and found out that the team had won 53-42! Everyone let out a cheer, and it made for a great night! The surgery was necessary because a stitch had come apart inside by the bladder and had formed an abscess, and it was the start of gangrene, which thankfully strong antibiotics started working on for him. He was very sick and ended up in the hospital six weeks. Mom stayed there the whole time and whenever we played a game, she would wear a Cherokee sweatshirt and soon all the nurses and doctors knew when we would be playing. She also had her car there and would go to the vehicle and see if she could hear the scores of the games.

I later called Coach Boettcher who said she was nervous and one of their players hit two 3's to start the game. She was panicked what to do and looked at Coach Blair. He said, "That girl hasn't hit anything all year; she's bound to start missing!" That player only made one more shot the rest of the game!

Throughout my coaching career, I have been blessed to have had great assistant coaches who are not only passionate about sports but also passionate about helping young people grow and become great citizens in the future. I've tried to give my assistants plenty of responsibilities and then tried to stay out of their way and let them do their jobs. Too many head coaches want to micromanage everything, which fails to grow confidence in assistants. If a head coach has to miss a game or a practice, the routine should stay the same and everything should continue as usual. **Great programs don't need coaches in order to be successful.**

Eventually, Dad continued to heal and made it home, and we continued to win games. The folks were unable to travel to games but because of KCHE Radio and the great John O'Connor, they could listen to every game on the radio. There were times when the game would not come in on the radio in the house, and it would come in better in the car, so they would sit in the car with some snacks and listen to the game. Even when it was winter and cold out, the car was running so the game could be heard!

My mom shared a story from an earlier year where a game wasn't coming in on the radio, even in the car. So, they decided to start driving toward Cherokee which was an hour away to see if it would come in. They kept driving, and it still wasn't coming in. Eventually, they looked ahead and could see Cherokee. By that time, they kept going but instead of heading to the gym where we were playing at the time, they drove around our house, and headed home. Mom said they were too embarrassed to stop! It's amazing she even told me the truth!

Our record grew to 16-0 as we headed to a clash with the dreaded Western Christian. It was at home, and a win would surely wrap up the conference title as they were the only team with one loss. Unfortunately, I picked a bad time to get as sick as I had ever been with a high fever, aches, and chills. The day of the game, I stayed home in the morning and came back at noon so I could coach but knew I wasn't in very good shape.

Who knows what I said in huddles or in the locker room during the game as I don't remember much other than we did not play very well. The opposing team was really pumped, and we lost the game. I went home right after the game, and I remember my temp was over 103 degrees! I missed the next two school days and despite still not feeling the best, went to school on Friday as we were to play at Emmetsburg.

For one of the few times in my career, I drove to a game, and Margo went along. I knew I would need to head home again right after the game. Fortunately, we played a great game and beat Hall of Fame coach Ted Riley by a large margin, jumped in the car, and headed back home. About 10 miles out of Emmetsburg, I was cruising at nearly 70 miles an hour as Margo was now not feeling well, and I wasn't doing cartwheels either. I came over a hill, and there was a police officer. You know what happened next. On came the red lights! I pulled over and when he came over, he said, "Did you know you were speeding?" I said, "Yes, I was. I am sick, my wife is sick, and we need to get home." He looked at me and exclaimed, "Thanks for our honesty: I'll put you down for 64 and get you out of here. Don't speed on the way home." He wrote me up and off we went. That was my first ever speeding ticket, but it could have been worse!

We finished off the regular season with three more wins to end the regular season at 20-1. Our good friends from Emmetsburg knocked off Western Christian in the last game to give us the conference title outright. What an accomplishment from 4-18 to a conference title! Enthusiasm was at an all time high, and we were anxious to start tournaments.

The state didn't do us any favors as we did not have any home games in the postseason and had a number of high win teams including Western Christian in our region. We won our first game comfortably at Pocahontas, and then played on a neutral court against an 18-3 Okoboji team with a 6'3", 6'1", and 6'0" front line. I remember the officiating being a "bit" questionable. OK, it wasn't very good in my mind and both teams shot a lot of free throws. We were down by 10 at halftime, and everything was going against us. However, we cranked the press up in the second half, our crowd was off the charts, and we found a way to win by two! There was no rest for the weary though as we were off to play Ft. Dodge St. Edmunds who was 18-4 at Manson, just a few miles out of Ft. Dodge. Our fans got there early like usual and outnumbered the St. Ed's fans. Despite a chilly night of shooting, we again found a way to win, 41-36. It was onto sub-state competition!

The final game to get to state was in Spencer. We had expected our opponent to be Western Christian again, but Sioux Center had beaten them in the second round so we played the Warriors. There was a game ahead of us that day. George-Little Rock earned its way to state so I felt that was a good omen! Also, our first state trip at Newell-Fonda was won in Spencer so I was happy to be there. I had asked Coach Blair to sit on the bench with us (he didn't do that during the season), and he said, "I don't want to mess anything up!" I told him when we made state, he was sitting with us no matter what. His teams had only made it to state once, and I knew it meant a lot to him. Plus, he had been a huge part of our success.

Obviously, we had played at Spencer before so we felt good about that, but when we walked in the gym, the GLR game was going on, and it was packed and LOUD! I immediately sensed our players were VERY nervous and did what I could to keep the mood light. This isn't life and death, I told them; we have to earn it, etc. I then remember someone saying, "Coach, did you see how many people are out there?"

The Sioux Center fans were right behind us, and some of them were let's just say not so friendly. I clearly remember some of them yelling, "Sit down coach" at me and my wife clearly yelling at them, "He doesn't have to sit down; he's the coach. Move if you don't like it!" Most people see my wife as a quiet, reserved person. I've been told at games, she turns into something much more than that and is my biggest defender! That should have told me right there that we were going to struggle, and when the game started, we certainly did. Communication was difficult, we had trouble scoring, turned the ball over a lot, and were very tentative, but our press got us some easy baskets to lead 20-18 at halftime. Surely, both teams would loosen up and play better in the second half, right?

Unfortunately, the answer was no. We burned the nets for a whopping three points in the third quarter but fortunately, held them to nine so we only trailed 27-23 after three quarters. The fourth quarter was as intense as you can imagine with incredible back and forth action. With less than a minute left and the score tied, one of our sophomores hit a free throw to take the lead and one of our

Before the Sioux Center game to go to state

freshmen hit two free throws to put us up 32-29 with five seconds left! We took a timeout at that point. I distinctly remember the public address announcer saying at that point, "Everyone MUST stay off the floor at the end of the game for the safety of the players." Remember that here in a second. As a coach, that is a situation where you have a lot of options. Do you foul, do you press, do you back off, etc? I have never fouled when up three as I am always worried about girls failing to block out and the other team getting the rebound! We decided to press but keep them in front of us.

Sioux Center threw the ball into their point guard who dribbled through most of our defense to the three point arc, pulled up, and took the shot as I heard the horn. The ball went in to tie the game. Wait...her foot was across the line...the horn went off first...it can't be, I thought. I looked over to the officials, and they were waving it off and leaving the floor; we had won the game! Watching tape later, both calls were correct, but what an ending!

Once the officials called the game, the senior brother of my point guard sprinted onto the floor, picked up his sister, and tossed her in the air! He was soon to be followed by our huge student section! So much for following the rules. It was a surreal moment. All of that work and here we were, going to state! I remember bear-hugging my wife and then being awarded the state banner amongst all of the students. I held it up in the air and then took it to our fans to enjoy. As I tried to catch my breath, I had one thought. If only the folks could have seen this! I knew they were listening, so I made my way up to John O'Connor for the post game interview. I'm not sure what I said, but I remember being teary-eyed and saying, "Dad and Mom, we did it; this was for you!" We called them soon after and the joy in their voices was something I will never forget!

First trip to state in 2003

We had over a week to get ready for the state tournament. It was truly a crazy week with so many people wishing us well, so many events to organize, and oh, we had to get ready for a game! I truly think I got too caught up in everything and didn't do a good enough job helping our team prepare. We found out our opponent was unbeaten and the #2 ranked Hudson. As we scouted them, we realized they were really big and strong, which was not our strength. We knew it was going to be a tough matchup, but we thought our press would give them trouble.

Game day came, and I could sense again the nervousness of the team and this time, we could not overcome the jitters. Our crowd was amazing again, one of the biggest in any class! You always hear it's tough to shoot at state because Veterans Memorial Auditorium (Vets) was so big and had so much room behind each basket. Well, we proved that, going 9-45 from the field. Our defense kept us in it the first half as we only trailed 13-11. However, Hudson turned up the press in the third quarter, and we trailed 30-19. Despite our best efforts, we ended up losing 40-25, nearly setting a record for fewest points in a game.

Everyone was heartbroken, but what a season-from 4-18 to 24-2 with a state berth and conference championship. That season and team will always have a special place in my heart. It was my first state appearance as a head coach. Parents of the team were incredibly supportive, and many remain close friends even today. The community support was unbelievable, and they lived and died with everything we did. Finally, our players were kids I had taught in seventh grade, and many had played volleyball also, so we had all spent a lot of time together. They would have run through a wall for me, and I was blessed to be able to work with all of them. We lost three great seniors but expectations were high going into the next season. We had lots of experience coming back, and everyone expected the winning to continue.

CHAPTER 12

WORK FOR SUCCESS

Don't Take Success for Granted

The next season, we played Newell-Fonda in the first game of the season at a tournament in Spencer. That was an odd game as my great friend, Coach Maske, had retired so it was strange to see Newell-Fonda basketball without him. However, his replacement, Dick Jungers (who would go on to win state softball and basketball titles later in his career) had the Mustangs playing typical NF basketball, and they led us 68-55 with 1:45 left. I was about to sub everyone, but we put on one last push with the press. Suddenly, two straight 3's got us back in the game. Newell-Fonda missed some free throws, and we were down by only one. They missed another free throw and our point guard drove the lane, and hit a 15' jumper at the buzzer to win the game! I've been fortunate to have a lot of teams come back from big deficits before but nothing like that with such a short amount of time left! **It does remind you to make sure players are fighting until the very end of the game. We have always told players that it takes 32 minutes every night, no matter what the circumstances are.** That's another life lesson-**you can't quit in anything if you want to be successful in it.** I have been so blessed to have players who buy into this concept and give it everything they have until the game is over. Those who succeed in life do the same thing.

I had concerns after the NF game as our defense was very porous against a smaller school, and we turned it over a lot. Until the end, our energy level was not where it needed to be, and it seemed like we just took for granted that we were going to win the game. I hoped that wasn't a trend. We went on to win our first three games before Sheldon beat us at home at the buzzer on an out of bounds play that I still remember to this day. We knew what they were going to do and should have played zone. Instead, I stayed in man-to-man and watched them make a layup at the buzzer.

From talking to other coaches, I think we all remember games and plays like that throughout our careers. Yes, you remember the great moments, but those heart-wrenching plays that make your team lose a game, and you mess something up stay with you forever. Unfortunately, I would have more of those to come in my career. Read on to see other examples of what coaches experience.

We did get on a roll mid-season and stood at 12-2 going into a rematch with

Sheldon on the road. We were pumped to play them again and knew this was a huge game in the conference as Sheldon and Western Christian (again!) were battling us at the top, and we had to go to WC the next game. It was at that point of the season that injuries started setting in, and our play was not at a high standard, even though our effort didn't waiver. We had numerous opportunities to put Sheldon away but missed several free throws and ended up losing in double overtime.

We turned around three days later and traveled to Sheldon to play Western at their gym. They were incredibly tall that year (OK, sorry, they were tall every year!) and they took it to us by over 20 points. We knew the conference was lost and with just a few regular season games left, the season was on the line. The next night we set a school record in points with 88 against Alta, but the rest of the season was a struggle. We lost to Le Mars and Spencer and finished tied for third in the conference, four games behind Western. Not what we were expecting, but we thought our experience would pay off in tournament play despite another tough road to state.

We won our first tournament game easily and then got matched up again with Okoboji, a team we had played in the same round the previous year and was 23-1 on the season. It was apparent from the beginning that they were eager for revenge and definitely outplayed and outcoached us throughout the game. I clearly remember a large number of fouls being called and our tallest player fouling out early in the fourth quarter which made things really difficult. As I think back to many games like this, especially early in my career, I spent too much time worrying what the officials were calling instead of focusing on doing my job and getting my kids in the right position to win. Obviously, I am very passionate about what I do, but spending too much time worrying about something I have no control over has probably lost my team some games over the years. I think I have gotten better with this as I have gotten older, but I deeply regret some of the decisions I made earlier in my career.

We ended up losing that game by nine which was a huge disappointment to the coaches, players, and community. This ended up to be Coach Blair's last game coaching as he retired that spring, and I was honored to have him on the bench with us, albeit in defeat. That season was a good reminder to **never take things for granted and that there are no guarantees that everything will turn out the way you want.** I think everyone including myself became a little too complacent before that season and just expected everything to come together like it had the previous year. **Every season is different, and you have to bring the same energy and passion to every one.**

I also think everyone felt a lot of pressure that season to win, and I was a part of that as well. I always talk about how important a "fun factor" is on successful teams, and I think I forgot about that too often during the season.

High school athletes rarely perform at their best when incredible pressure is put on them. If you had to pin me down on my biggest regrets in coaching, one would definitely be putting too much emphasis on winning and getting too upset when things didn't go right. If only we could have a mulligan on our pasts!

CHAPTER 13

ALWAYS SEE THE BIG PICTURE

Life and Sports Aren't Always Fair

Going into the 2004-05 season, we knew we were only going to lose two seniors and if we could stay healthy, we should be as good as anyone in the state. I remember putting on the season ending packet that "You haven't heard the last of us yet!" How true that was!

The 2004-05 basketball season arrived, and we hit the court running full speed. We added a couple of freshmen to our rotation and had some other players step up their play as well. We opened the season by drilling Pocahontas Area by 37; they would go on to make the 2A state tournament later in the season. An early key was going to Sheldon and Western Christian in back-to-back games and beating them by a combined 52 points. It was at that point that I considered the possibility that this team could go unbeaten. Their focus, dedication, and drive were unmatched!

We rolled into Christmas unbeaten and beat every team by at least 14 points. We moved into the rankings at #8 but knew the schedule would be tough. Spirit Lake only had one loss in the conference and Battle Creek-Ida Grove was coming up with only one loss as well. Also, as great as it was to be beating everyone by large margins, we hadn't been tested, and we knew we weren't going to win every game easily the rest of the season.

The Spirit Lake game was as tight as expected and went down to the wire. Our teams played similar styles, and their coach, BJ Mayer, and I had similar, "passionate" coaching styles, so it was like playing ourselves. They cut the lead to two late in the game, but we made free throws and won by six. It was a good learning experience for the rest of the season.

Our next game was at BC-IG, a team we had built a great rivalry with as the schools were close, and we played a lot in the summer. Right before the game, we had found out that BC-IG was in our tournament region, and we would have to win there in tournaments so at least we would have a game under our belts in that gym before tournament action began.

We discovered heading into the game that one of our players would likely go over the 1000 point mark for her career. She would be only the third player to do that at Cherokee and was the first one I had ever coached. She had no idea so we decided to surprise her after the game. I let her family know so they could be there and support her. The other issue was letting BC-IG know and see if it was OK to do something after the game. I contacted their coach, Pat Miller, and he was incredibly obliging. He had coached our player during the summer on some select teams and knew the family as well. It was a tight game, but we pulled away to win by 19, and the ceremony after the game was just what I'd hoped it would be. Although basketball is a team game, I've always thought honoring big, individual accomplishments like 1000 points was incredibly important as it respects the time and efforts those players have put in as well as what their families have done over time to support their kids. **Team accomplishments come first, but finding ways to recognize individuals is a must as well.**

Every time I have had a player reach a milestone and had to visit with an opposing coach about having something, they have been extremely gracious and willing to help out. I'm sure many non-coaches reading this think there is a lot of jealousy and hard feelings by coaches against each other in this profession. I have found that probably 99% of the time, this has not been the case. Coaches are obviously very competitive people so during games and matches, there may be moments of "anger" toward an opposing coach. However, once the games are over, I think we all understand what the opposing coach is going through so we help each other out as much as we can. If I have a question about another team, a situation, or need a game tape, you can bet there are coaches willing to help. I believe there is a real "fraternity" among coaches, and we all know how tough our jobs are. Everyone sees what we do. Whether we are at our best or at our worst, fans at activities, including parents, can judge how well we are doing. It is many times a thankless job that most of us don't do for the money but do for the kids and for the love of sports.

I have been fortunate to be part of a profession with so many quality people who have become great friends down the road. There are too many names to mention here, but I have been blessed to work with and compete against so many incredible people. I have learned so much from those coaches and when times are tough, I know I have those coaches to rely on!

We rolled on after the BC-IG game, winning the last eight regular season contests by at least 15 points, including an 18-point win at Spirit Lake to wrap up the conference title and an unbeaten regular season. We were ready for tournaments, but we also knew it was not going to be easy. We had only been tested a couple of times. We would have to win at BC-IG, and #5 Hinton was waiting on the other side of the region.

We defeated Marcus-Meriden-Cleghorn easily in the first game and then headed to Ida Grove to take on BC-IG whose record was 19-3. It was a packed house and our fans did their usual great job of coming early and packing our side of the gym! In those days, the girls' union in charge of athletics was very straightforward that the team at the top of the bracket in tournaments was the "home" team and would sit to the right of the score table along with wearing white uniforms; there were no exceptions to this. For the BC-IG game, we were on top of the bracket and the home team, despite the game being at Ida Grove. Coach Miller from BC-IG had contacted me about making a change and keeping them in white and on the right side. If we had both agreed to it, it could have been changed. I felt like the rules should be followed to a T, and honestly, I knew it was a disadvantage to them to be in a different uniform and on a different bench than what they were used to in their gym. I'm sure Coach Miller still holds a grudge about that, but he would go on to win a state title and have a couple of runner-up finishes so he did pretty well for himself.

As for the game, the opposing team took it to us at the beginning and led by five after a quarter as they played well, and we were very tentative. However, the last three quarters, we turned up the press and took the ball aggressively to the basket. Late free throws helped seal the win, 65-55. We were excited to get past that one, and through a quirk of scheduling, knew we would be at home for the next game.

Conference rival Sheldon was up next and interestingly enough, they were on top of the bracket, so we had to wear black and sit on the other bench for the game. That and the fact we had beaten Sheldon by 22 and 30 points in our first two games made me extremely nervous. I also knew their coach, Kris Groff (also Sheldon's volleyball coach and a great friend) would have some tricks up his sleeve to get ready for us. Tricks was the right word as Sheldon came out in "junk" defenses and took away our two best offensive players. We struggled to score, and the pressure mounted. We led by nine at halftime but early in the third quarter, they made a run and nearly tied the game. However, we made a 15-0 run at the end of the quarter, highlighted by one of our freshmen hitting a shot from nearly midcourt at the buzzer! We rolled in the fourth and won by 30.

The last two games really point out the importance in athletics of just playing your game and not getting caught up in distractions and other abnormalities that may occur. **Control what you can control and don't get caught up in claiming something is "not fair."** Most of the time, situations even out, and if we are worrying about things we can't fix, we will never play or coach the best we are capable of. This is so true in life also!

Hinton was knocked off earlier in tournaments, so our opponent in the game to go to state was the same as two years ago, Sioux Center. The game was in Le Mars where we had previously played, so that and having beaten Sioux Center two years ago (they had some of the same players as well) gave us some confidence, but we knew it would be a tough game. We played a good first half and led by eight at halftime. We started the second half on a 15-0 run (must have been a great speech, right?), and it looked like we could relax and enjoy the ride to state! Unfortunately, they fought back and cut it to single digits before we once again hit key free throws and won by 11.

We were headed back to Des Moines with a 25-0 record and a #4 ranking! There was also a different feeling this time than the previous state trip. We were thrilled with getting back to state, but there was still "unfinished business." Two years before, I think we were happy to just make it to state and got caught up in all of the hoopla. This time, we wanted to win three more games and make history. Although we were excited during the week leading up to state, our focus was clear, and we had great practices. Our first game was on Tuesday morning at 10:00 a.m. which was a concern, but it would also give us more time to warm-up and shoot at the baskets at Vet's Auditorium. 2005 was a special state tournament as that was the last year games were played at Vet's. The next year, everything was being moved across the street to the brand new Wells Fargo Arena. As a history major and sports buff, being one of the last four state champions to be awarded at Vet's was a big deal, and we talked to the team about making history.

Game day arrived, and it was clear we were ready to go. Our opponent was Carroll Kuemper whose record was only 14-11, but I knew how tough their conference was as they were in the same league as Atlantic. Watching films, they weren't real tall but were very aggressive and very athletic. There were no jump balls to start a game during that time so Kuemper had the first possession. As they threw the ball in, I turned on the bench to grab my water. As I was doing that, I heard a loud roar from our crowd (who turned out in HUGE numbers again!). I turned to look and our point guard had stolen the ball and was laying it in for a 2-0 lead. Not a bad way to start the game! We never looked back and won 62-39. We forced 35 turnovers and had 24 steals which is still a state tournament record for one game! It was great to get the monkey off our back of winning at state. Facing us was #1 ranked Grundy Center with two division one players, one 6'3" going to Iowa, and one 6'0" going to Drake. The four teams left in 2A were the top-ranked teams so the girls' union had it right. That didn't make it any easier!

The game was scheduled to start at 2:30, but the game ahead of ours went into overtime so we had a long wait. I did not note any tension at all, and I distinctly remember our kids dancing to various songs played during timeouts and generally having a great time. One thing you never know about state games is who you will have for officials. Many times, smaller schools get officials who usually did larger school games and vice versa. Basically, you never had officials that reffed during the regular season so that it was fair to everyone.

As we took the court for warm-ups for the Grundy Center game, I saw the officials walking toward me. They are two officials from who we had a number of times during the season, and were obviously well known to our fans and us. As they walked toward me, before I could say a word, one of them stated, "I know, Curt, we are confused too and have no idea why we are reffing your game." We joked about it, and they moved on. I didn't think anything of it at the time, but it was to become a factor as the game went on.

The game started, and we got off to a slow start. Their height and very physical play were hard to overcome. Our tallest player got in early foul trouble, and the opposing team seemed to get away with a lot of push offs, but nothing was called. They outrebounded us by 15, and that was a big factor as well. We were down by seven at halftime, but Grundy Center started pulling away in the third and went up by 13 late in the quarter. My frustration level with the officiating was rising as well, but fortunately, the team kept fighting in typical fashion and a combination of our press, 3-pointers, and free throws got us within two. With less than 15 seconds left, one of our sophomores hit a jumper, sending us to overtime and our crowd into a frenzy; the game was ours!

Overtime was a free throw contest to start and was still tied with less than 40 seconds left. Grundy Center missed a shot, and their center pushed, and then went over the back of two of our players. At least that is what I saw! She got the rebound, made the basket, and put them up two. If a foul was called there, our best free throw shooter had two at the other end. Game tape later showed a clear foul, but none was called. Oh well. We came down the floor, took a good shot and appeared to get fouled. Video later showed the same, but nothing was called. They got the rebound, and we had to foul. They made one of two, and our last shot missed; we were on the short end 66-63.

Devastated cannot begin to describe the feelings the team and I had. One of the toughest parts of coaching is talking to a team when their season, and in many instances, their careers have ended. I've had almost 30 years of practice, and this speech never gets easier. If you had a group of kids who didn't really care, it wouldn't be very hard. I've been fortunate that almost all of my teams truly cared about what we did so they take the end of the seasons very hard.

This speech was one of the hardest I ever gave. I truly felt we should have won, I felt the officiating had taken it away from us, and yet, complaining about the officiating wasn't going to make them feel better. I told them how proud I was of them and how much I cared about them. I said that this was tough, but we all needed to own up to it and move on, and that there were more important things in life than winning games. They had done everything they could, and they needed to hear that from me.

One of the interesting parts of being at state is talking to the media after the games. When you win, it is great, because there is a lot to share! However, after a loss, it is as tough as it gets. The state always wants a couple players to come with the head coach and talk to the media. What a difficult spot for a person that age but what a life lesson as well. As the two players and I were walking to the location for our interview with the media, both were sobbing and in tears. We stopped for a minute, and I reminded them to remember how great this whole experience had been, and to be gracious in defeat as they were representing our school and their families as well.

I have been blessed at my basketball stops to have announcers like Chris Boeckman in Storm Lake, Jim Field in Atlantic, John O'Connor in Cherokee, and Tim Fleming in Mason City who have allowed athletes to talk live on the radio after games. I have also had some of the best newspaper people like Jamie Knapp and the Gallagher brothers in Storm Lake, Paul Struck and Jeff Benson in Cherokee, all of the newspaper guys in Sioux City, and Kirk Hardcastle and Jared Patterson in Mason City work with athletes and not only showcase their talents but give them an opportunity to work on communication skills they need the rest of their lives. Add in television people like AJ Ellingson from Mason City who put together great bits for the public and spend countless hours working on their stories, and you can see I feel blessed with the media my players and I have worked with through sports seasons.

I know some coaches feel working with the media is not needed and would rather not do it. I totally disagree. The high majority of the media does a great job of reporting on teams and without coaches' help, players will not get the credit they deserve. I know the media has a job to do and my job is to help them in any way I can. We both have thankless jobs sometimes, and the public doesn't always appreciate the work that coaches and the media do, but if we aren't working together and doing what's right, it's the kids that get hurt. I will always be a big supporter of the media!

As the two players and I met the media, I could hear the players' comments. I couldn't have been more proud! They spoke with composure and class and couldn't have represented themselves and their team any better. What an amazing thing for young adults to be able to do! I was literally blasted with questions about the officiating like what did you think of it, did you think they missed a lot of calls, did it affect the outcome of the game? My response each time was, "I don't have a comment about the officiating." The press kept prodding and kept the same response. I didn't want to say what I was feeling at the time; yes, I think it affected the outcome, and why did the state have officials from our conference? We should have won, however, I felt it was best to have no response. I needed to follow the example of my players, and I needed to be an example for everyone. If you want maybe a different view of things, Paul Struck with our local paper wrote a very interesting article about officiating at the game. Paul always has a way with words and is always honest to a T!

I truly at the time and to this day, do not hold any grudges or ill will against those officials. Both were/are great guys, with great integrity, and great knowledge of the game. Did they have a tough game? According to my observations and from watching the game tape, yes they did. However, how many tough games have I had as a coach? Too many to mention. Did they purposely want us to lose-no way; they were doing their job. Did they purposely try to make sure they weren't coming across as favoring us since they were so close to Cherokee? I probably thought so at the time, but I doubt that as well. The state put them in a really tough spot.

I have obviously had some questions with regards to officiating at times throughout my career, but overall, I have great admiration for officials and the impossible job they have. I have officiated a number of youth basketball tournaments, and it is easy to see how calls can get missed with the speed of the game. It's always easier to officiate from the stands anyway, right? I think I have gotten better over time with regards to how I work with officials. I must admit I watch a lot of games and see coaches get away with a lot of things and nothing is said to them, but when I say anything, I get told to "sit down and shut up, Coach!" No matter what an official may say to me, as long as they hustle and work hard at the job, I will respect what they do.

After the players and I finished talking to the media, we were literally told to hurry up and get out of the area as they had to clean everything up for the night games. I hadn't seen my wife nor my family (my parents had made the game) so we were told where they would be and headed to that area. After some searching, we finally found the family. I found out that the security guards had been quite rude and were forcing them to leave, but Mom had gotten into an argument with a security guard and told him in no uncertain terms, "My son is the coach, and I am NOT leaving until we see him!" LOL!! How funny would it have been for the media to have to report that the coach's mom was arrested after the game, and it didn't have anything to do with the officiating!

The team stayed for the championship game on Friday night, and we saw Grundy Center win the title, which was another gut punch to all of us. However, I took the lead from Coach Maske when I was at Newell-Fonda and made sure that we had fun the rest of our stay. Kids usually recover faster from losses than coaches do anyway so we made it a memorable finish to the season.

The 2004-05 Cherokee girls' basketball team will go down as one of the best in school history. They were definitely a great group of kids and parents who came together with a common purpose to produce memories that will last a lifetime. I have remained friends with many of these players and parents through social media to this day, and it's incredible to watch the players grow up into amazing adults with families of their own. Nothing gives me more satisfaction as a coach.

How do you top a season like that? We actually took a good shot at it during the 2005-06 season. We had lost an amazing senior class along with my fantastic assistant, Coach Boettcher, but still had three huge cogs from the previous year's team and had some promising newcomers as well. This would also be the first state tournament at Wells Fargo Arena so we wanted to be one of the first teams to play at state there. Our tournament classification changed as we moved up to 3A, which I thought at the time might be a good thing as there were a bunch of excellent 2A teams in our area, and you only had to win three games to go to state in 3A instead of the usual four games required in 2A.

We charged out of the gates 8-0, winning each of those games by at least 10 points. However, we knew that our last game before Christmas was at Spirit Lake, a team with a great coach in BJ Mayer with a ton of young talent. We had beaten them the previous year, but they returned almost everyone, and I knew they would be gunning for us. Spirit Lake was certainly ready for us and drilled us 78-62 in a game that was not close. They were just faster, more athletic, better coached, and wanted it more than we did. It was the first time in a few years that someone had taken it to us like that. Fortunately, we had the holiday break coming up and had time to regroup. I've always been a fan of the quote by former Secretary of State Colin Powell who once said, "Get mad, then get over it." Although we were disappointed in the loss, Spirit Lake was the only team ahead of us in the conference, and we knew that if we won the rest of our games, we would have them at our place at the end of the season and could at least tie for the conference championship.

I am a big believer in the importance of finding little ways to motivate my teams and myself to continue to work and get better even if things aren't looking good. It gives you a reason to keep working and keep a positive attitude. **Sports teach you to move on in life quickly. Otherwise, you will be left behind and in a worse position than you were before.**

We won our first two games after break easily and headed into a huge non-conference game with our rivals BC-IG. They were unbeaten and ranked fourth in 2A. As close as our games had been the past few years and with their entire lineup back, we knew it was going to be a battle. They also had a Division 1 starter who went on to later star at Iowa State. BC-IG jumped on us 8-6 after one quarter, and their best player dominated the entire first half. We decided to change defenses into a box and one that we had never tried before and had seldom practiced. It definitely frustrated her and their team, and we slowly got back into it. With our crowd roaring its approval, we hit a three-pointer at the end of the third quarter to take our first lead by three and went on to win by five.

I knew this was a huge win and hoped it would drive us forward, which it did. We won our next seven games, including a tough road win at Sioux City

Heelan, coming back from being down six at halftime in a gym affectionately called the "Pit." It is an old school-type gym with a stage on one side, and the crowd right on top of you! The concession stand that night was also on the stage so the smell of hotdogs and popcorn was evident throughout the gym.

That led us to the rematch with Spirit Lake. They had won all of their games but had an upset loss in the conference since then, and we each had a couple of conference games left, but it was clear this was for the conference title. Our confidence was high, and we were playing at home so we knew that would give us an extra boost. I really wanted this for our seniors. Two of these athletes had played for four years, and another who had come back out as a senior and had really given us a boost where we needed it. Unfortunately, it was not meant to be. Despite a packed house with screaming Braves fans, we turned it over 20 times despite no press from Spirit Lake and got caught up in the moment with a lot of nerves and a lot of forced shots, especially late in the game. We somehow led by a point after three quarters but couldn't hold on as Spirit Lake hit a short shot with a few seconds left to win by two.

I don't think I coached a good game and let my emotions get the best of me. My players needed me at my best, and I did not come through. After the game, I took a bit to put all of my items, including our stat device in my bag like usual. Right before entering the locker room, I took my bag and flung it across the hall against a wall. Immediately, I heard a loud crash and knew I had broken the stat device...oops. At the time, I was frustrated at the players for losing that opportunity, but ultimately, I was just as much or more to blame than they were. I ended up buying a new device with my own money.

I think I have done a better job over the years of controlling my emotions both in the classroom and on the court, and I believe my wife deserves the most credit for that. She never questions anything about what I do on the court, and when I get home from a game or practice, we never talk about what happened. I've developed a life outside school and basketball, and we all need to do that. If our jobs become our lives, we will never truly "win." **Perspective in life is vital to living a successful one.**

We won our last two regular season games to finish 20-2, which was pretty remarkable with players we had lost the last year. We knew Spirit Lake stood in our way to get back to state, but we were excited to hopefully meet them again as we all know that "it is hard to beat someone three times during a season!"

An easy win over Algona at home started our tournament run, and then we were forced by the girls' union for some reason to play Le Mars a team we had beaten twice on a neutral court in Storm Lake. Also, for some reason, they put the Le Mars students directly behind our bench so they were in our ears the entire game! One of our players had a 64 ounce water bottle that she used, so whenever she got the ball, they yelled "Big Gulp, Big Gulp!" Very creative, I thought! We actually had a lot of fun with that. There were a couple of fans in particular who were yelling at me most of the night, telling me to "sit down" and mentioning my "ugly basketball tie." It may not have been an accident that I just happened to stand directly in front of those fans much of the game so they probably had a right to complain that they couldn't see.

Despite a tough game and a lot of fouls being called (we shot 44 free throws!), we won by 14 to advance to the regional finals. At the end of the game, the same fans kept yelling at me. I had not said anything to them during the game, and usually never do. However, I will always support my players! With 20 seconds left, I finally went over to those students and said, "You might want to look at the scoreboard!" Their student section erupted, and the two most vocal students high-fived me as the buzzer sounded!

I generally love to see students support their teams in great fashion. It adds so much to the environment and makes it a bigger deal to the players. I have been very fortunate that everywhere I have been, our students have been huge supporters of my teams. You hear sometimes that girls' sports aren't supported very well, but I think we have been a counter to that. I tell players that if you want more fans, play the game the right way, get excited yourself, and people will support you. In the back of my mind, I want to make sure that our teams are worth supporting by playing an exciting type of ball, no matter what the sport, and by demanding 100% effort all of the time by players and coaches. If we are going to do something, we are going to do it right! I am so appreciative of the amazing support my teams have received.

As expected, Spirit Lake also made the regional final, and we were scheduled to play in Spencer. We had a good game plan going in, and we felt confident it was our turn to win. We played with great poise early and jumped ahead 32-23 at halftime. However, Coach Mayer mixed up some defenses and the momentum shifted. Our all-conference point guard also got in foul trouble and fouled out with three minutes left. Despite a four-point lead after three quarters, and a seesaw fourth quarter, they took the lead by two with under 20 seconds to play.

After a deflection out of bounds, we ran a play and got it to our senior post inside the lane. She got the ball, went up, and in my view got clearly raked across the arm (video later shows that appeared to be the case), missed the shot, and they got the rebound. We fouled, they made one of two free throws, and the game was over. They beat us for a third time and wildly celebrated their trip to state. For the second time in two weeks, our hearts were ripped out after a loss. We had our chances and didn't come through. They had found a way to beat us three times and were the better team according to the records. I believe we should have won two of those games, but we just weren't good enough in pressure situations.

I think players are the reason that teams win or lose, but coaches play a bigger factor in the close games. Overall, my teams have done a great job in pressure situations, but I certainly feel like I let the team down that season and didn't make enough adjustments to ensure success. It was tough to see our seniors leave with three fantastic kids with great parents. What a legacy they had left; we were 89-13 during those years with two conference titles, two state appearances, and a bunch of near misses. I knew it would be hard to keep that kind of success going, and it was!

CHAPTER 14

HIGH EXPECTATIONS EQUAL SUCCESS

Better Luck This Time?

The 2006-07 season arrived with continued high expectations, although I had my concerns. We did have some experience returning, but I was concerned about our depth and also how hard our players were working to get better. Our younger players were great kids but had not been as dedicated to getting better as some of our previous classes. Looking back, I feel I was a part of the problem as well. I had started to become complacent and our off-season program was not as dedicated as it could have been. **Sometimes when you have success, it's easy to take it for granted and assume that it is just going to continue, no matter how hard you work. Unfortunately, in sports, in business, and in life, the moment you become complacent is the moment you fall behind others. One of my favorite sayings is that you are either getting better or you are getting worse at what you are doing. You don't reach a certain point and stay there; you either keep climbing the mountain, or you start sliding down it.** Looking back, I feel this was a part of my life where I was sliding a bit.

Our 2006-07 season started on a down note as we had to travel to Sheldon and Western Christian, two teams we had dominated the last four years. They were ready for us, and we started the season 0-2. We bounced back before Christmas with a couple of wins and also had over a 30-point loss at Spencer and another 15-point loss at home against Spirit Lake. Even the wins were a struggle though, and we went into break at 3-5.

We started the second half of the season with a close loss at Estherville-Lincoln Central. Our next game was at old rival BC-IG, and I knew this had the makings of a disaster all over it, and it came true. They were obviously motivated and destroyed us in every part of the game. We couldn't handle their press, and they kept their starters in most of the game while continuing to press. 36 turnovers later, we had lost by 39, probably the worst loss of my career. Clearly, we felt they were trying to run up the score, and I subbed all of our kids in by early in the fourth quarter. That has always been my philosophy. If a game is out of hand, the bench is going to play, whether we are way ahead or way behind. It is frustrating to have opposing coaches keep their top kids in the whole game when the margin is huge, but each coach has to do what is best for his/her group.

One thing I get asked at times is if I've ever had a team score over 100 points in a game; the answer is no. The only times we have been close to that is when we are ahead of the opponent by a significant amount, and at that point, I will have our bench in the game. I'm sure if we would keep our starters in a whole game and continue to run and press like usual, we would have scored 100 by now. **Coaches shouldn't be in the business of trying to embarrass another team or another coach.** Certainly we have beaten teams by large margins in the past, and I have had a couple of occasions where opponents have accused me of running up the score. I would never tell my reserves to stop shooting or to stop playing good defense as they deserve the right to play. However, coaches can play a huge role in keeping a score within reason. The state has implemented recently a "mercy rule" where the clock runs continuously in the second half if the margin is more than 35 points. I think the rule is fine, but coaches need to control this themselves.

Coaches need to be role models for their teams, and this is true when games are close or when they are out of hand. Athletics are meant by nature to be ultra competitive, but there needs to be a time and place for compassion as well. Ultimately, wins and losses come down to the athletes, and as coaches, we are all going to have times where we are winning big and where we are losing big. How we handle those should say a lot about us.

After the BC-IG game, the rest of our regular season had continued ups and downs. We had six more losses and all but one were by more than 15 points which was very discouraging. Our kids played hard like always, but we had all sorts of problems scoring points and other teams were just better than we were. We did end the regular season with two wins but went into the tournament trail with an 8-13 record. We had dropped down to 2A and knew the post season would be difficult but hoped our experience would win out.

Fortunately, our first game against Hinton was at home and despite a lot of turnovers and being out-rebounded by eight, we pulled out an exciting win by seven. That led us to the district final at Unity Christian which was a team that had ended my volleyball seasons numerous times, and unfortunately, did the same this season for basketball. They held us to our lowest point total of the season, and their overall speed and athletic ability were too much for us as we went down 61-33.

That game pretty much typified the season. The players worked extremely hard and had a great attitude, but it wasn't enough. This was a tough way to end as I was very close to the five seniors who were in third grade when I first came to the district so I had seen them start at the very beginning of their athletic careers. All five also played volleyball so we had spent a lot of time together. Although the season was a tough one, there was a lot of hope for the future. The JV team had finished 17-1, and we had good classes coming up. I knew we had to change some things in order to get back on top and was ready to get back to work to make that happen. Little did I know that the Unity game would be my last at Cherokee.

CHAPTER 15

CHANGE IS INEVITABLE

Don't Be Afraid of Change

April 23, 2007, was a day that changed my life forever. I was at home working on some projects in our basement when I received a call from my superintendent at Cherokee. Margo had recently quit as the technology coordinator at the school, mainly because of disagreements with the superintendent, so we weren't exactly cordial. In a very excited voice (I wasn't sure how to take that!), he told me that the Mason City superintendent had called and wanted to visit with me about their head girls' basketball position. Even when I expressed pessimism about it, he exclaimed, "It would be a great position for you!" Margo and I had never talked about leaving Cherokee. We loved everything about the town, our friends, our house, my job, etc. However, this was a different position because MC was her hometown, her parents still lived there, and the town offered many amenities. We had been there numerous times, and I had followed their sports' teams casually since her parents were there. We decided to at least listen to what they had to say with no pressure about having to get the job since we loved where we were.

A time to interview was set up and before the interview, I did call Chad Jilek, the former coach who was moving on to Waukee, and I appreciated his honesty on the state of the program and what to look for in a position like this. He said there were a lot of good kids in the younger grades, and the potential for success was there. I also talked to a couple of other friends in the area, and they didn't sugar coat it. It was a tough job no matter who took it. There were a bunch of negatives, however. Most of the competition was in Des Moines, two hours away so there were a lot of long trips. Those schools were much better off than Mason City, and people didn't support the girls' program like they should. I decided to try and find out some things for myself.

Another coach I heard from was someone who had actually interviewed for the MC position and another head coaching position at the same time. He was offered both positions but decided to take the other job. When I talked to him, he was very high on the Mason City position; the other job just worked better for his family and living position. He went on to win a state title at that school so it worked out well for everyone.

The day of the interview, Margo and I decided to leave early and stop at a quilt shop along the way as my wife loves quilting. We had only told a few people of the interview and really had low expectations so it honestly wasn't a big deal to us. At the quilt shop (it was out in the country), we saw another Cherokee plate. I stayed in the car (quilting is not my thing!) and when Margo came back, she said one of her friends from the quilting guild was there and wondered what we were doing there. She told her friend I had a meeting, which was true.

We got to Mason City a bit early so we drove around a bit to check out the town and be reminded of what was there. I have told this story to people many times, but one of the things I saw that got me the most excited was seeing that they had a Wendy's! I love Wendy's and love their frosties since Cherokee didn't have one, so that was one plus for Mason City!

Once we got to the school, I had a great meeting with Superintendent Keith Sersland, whose passion was contagious, and he made it clear they wanted me for the job. He told me they had talked to numerous people, including the head of the girls' union, and he had recommended me for the position. Keith said girls' basketball had struggled at Mason City, and they had never won the conference or made it to state, but they wanted a winning program and would support me in whatever fashion needed. It was a very powerful message!

The next meeting was at the middle school as there was a teaching position open. I interviewed with Principal TJ Jumper and Assistant Principal Tim Johnson. I was impressed with the knowledge and passion they both displayed and with all of the initiatives they had implemented. TJ was quite a bit younger than me, and I knew it would be different having a principal that young, but he had a great sports background (he had been a high JUMPER in college at the University of Illinois) so there was an immediate connection. I felt comfortable that it would be a good fit to teach there.

The last meeting was with the Athletic Director Dan Delaney. We had a great meeting although I was discouraged to hear that he was retiring at the end of the school year. He did tell me that his replacement was Bob Kenny, who had been an administrator for West Des Moines Dowling, but I had known him as the long-time successful wrestling coach at Lakes Conference rival Emmetsburg, so I knew I would have a lot of support. Dan had similar views to Mr. Sersland and was confident that a winning program could be build in MC.

I had requested the chance to meet with some returning players to gauge what the goals and expectations were from them. I expected Dan to sit in on the meeting but instead he introduced me to the players and said to let him know when we were done. OK then! It was a great talk. They were awesome kids, and I felt an immediate connection with them. They asked great questions, and I had a lot of questions for them. I believe they were most impressed by my goofy basketball tie.

I guess I should explain that for as long as I have been a head basketball coach, I have worn basketball ties when I wear a coat and tie to games. I don't remember when it happened, but I believe when I was an assistant at Newell-Fonda, I got one as a Christmas gift. It seemed to be a hit with people, and I started to get more of them as gifts. Over the years, I added other "eccentric" ties, but those have pretty much stayed in the closet lately! My dad was always a big fan of my basketball ties so it was a tradition that just started, and I haven't had a reason to change it. A lot of coaches have superstitions when it comes to games, but I do not. Fortunately, my wife has a great sense of fashion so I at least match when I coach games.

After the player meeting, Mr. Delaney took me on a tour of the school. The gym was a big, older structure with a lot of seating, and it was clear it could be a huge home court advantage. It was very intriguing to think about playing there and what it would be like if the place was packed. Mr. Delaney reminded me that the superintendent had asked me to stop by his office one more time before we left town. His comments were very succinct; he had checked in with everyone who talked to me during the day, and they all wanted me to come to Mason City. He went through what my contract would look like with a big jump in salary, increased benefits, and a chance to do something great. It was inspiring and overwhelming in many aspects. Mr. Sersland said he would call when I got home, and I said we would need time to consider everything.

I really hadn't talked to Margo much during the day as she was off doing other things in her hometown. Once I got in the car, I said, "The job is mine if I want it. What do you think?" To say she was stunned would be an understatement. As we headed to Clear Lake and the interstate to head home, I told Margo it was time to make a list of the positives of going to Mason City and the positives of staying in Cherokee. This wouldn't be a final decision-maker, but I thought having a visual of what we were facing would be good for both of us. After a lot of talking and creating our list, she showed me the piece of paper. There were many more positives on the side of going to Mason City than there were staying in Cherokee. It has nothing to do with Cherokee because we had a great thing going there. It came down to all of the possibilities of going to Mason City.

Margo and I had a number of discussions the rest of the way home and honestly, a lot of people assume it was harder for me to think about leaving than it was for her. It was the other way around. She loved Cherokee, and she also knew the dynamic of being back "home" wasn't bound to be perfect either. The relationship with Margo and her parents had certainly had its share of ups and downs, and she is probably even less of a change person than I am, and I like to keep things as is most of the time.

We arrived back in Cherokee and hadn't been home for very long when the phone rang. It was Mr. Sersland. He wanted to officially offer me the position, and he hoped for an answer. As I had told him in Mason City, Margo and I needed to talk it over, I needed to talk it over with some Cherokee people, and I needed time to think. This was a huge decision, and we wanted to make sure it was the right decision.

One negative part of possibly moving to Mason City was being two hours away from my parents and much of my family. We had told them about the interview, and obviously they weren't doing cartwheels over the possibility. Dad especially seemed to be having a hard time with it. I told them they had an issue when I moved to Atlantic, and it all worked out fine and if we moved, it would be fine as well. However, I knew it wouldn't be the same.

The folks had been able to make it back to so many of my games especially with two conference opponents being 15 minutes away from them, and the fact they both had health issues previously and weren't getting any younger made it a much more agonizing decision. I was calmed by the fact my brothers, sister, and families were close to George and would be there as things came up. Since Margo was an only child, the fact that we would move to Mason City would be helpful down the road as her parents got older as well.

We were definitely leaning toward moving and that night, I talked to a few more friends and family to try and figure out what to do. After looking at everything, an overriding thought kept coming to me. I felt there was something more I could be doing and that my "legacy" was not complete. This was an opportunity to build another program and do something no one had ever done at Mason City. The fact they were a much bigger school and would compete against the biggest schools in the state never really bothered me. I thought the principles of basketball we taught at Cherokee were transferrable to bigger schools. As a competitor, the challenge of doing something that many people said was not doable was hard to overcome.

Obviously, I have left for a new position three different times, and I've been asked numerous times, how do you know it is time to move on? My answer is usually, I don't know; each case is unique. I think you have to list the pros and cons of each job, like we did with this move. You also have to look to the future and see if the new job is going to make your future better.

With coaching, if you have built a good program, you are going to leave good kids as I had to do in every stop. I'm a big believer, however, that wherever you end up, it is up to you to make it a "good" fit. I think generally there are good people everywhere, and if you do what you are supposed to and help make your new setting a better place, it doesn't matter as much where you go. That doesn't make a decision whether to move or not any easier, but it should never stop a person from looking to advance.

98

Margo and I woke up the next morning and I said, "We need to do this." I'm not sure she was 100% on board, but she had faith in me, and I think she knew what it meant to me. I hadn't signed a contract yet at Cherokee so I knew everything was going to work out with my contract. I called Mr. Sersland and Mr. Delaney first, and they were thrilled. That was the fun part; I knew the worst was yet to come.

I went to the high school first and talked to the office people, including our superintendent, who was thrilled (SURPRISE!) and our AD, Neil Phipps as well. His daughter had played volleyball for me and had been a basketball manager so we had a great relationship. He was an old military guy and as tough as they come, but also a fantastic people person. You could tell he was disappointed but was also happy for us. One thing I learned from Neil was the value of a short note to people to let them know you were happy for them or appreciated them. He was great at writing those notes, and ever since we moved to Cherokee, I still get a note from Coach Phipps on occasion. We all including myself need to do more of that!

From there, I went back to the middle school to tell my principal and the staff. There may have been nothing I was dreading more than that. I got there before school started and Mr. Weede, my principal, was in his office. We had talked about my interview in MC, and I think he had an idea of what was coming. I don't remember exactly what I said, but I believe it was, "I'm leaving." I could see tears forming in his eyes (and mine as well) as he thanked me for everything I had done, and he was so sorry to see me go. Wow, that made it even harder to leave as I knew it would be hard to replace that man in my life. What a people person he was and believed in his staff and his students to the core. I am forever grateful to have worked for this man who embodied so much of what is good in education today.

Telling my great friends on the middle school staff was difficult as well. I had developed a special bond with seventh grade math teacher Sally Knoben. Her daughter had played for me for three years. She and her husband Chuck were fantastic Braves supporters (you could always hear Chuck yell "REBOUND" during games!). Her parents were similar ages to my parents and were great supporters, and we obviously had many conversations being part of the seventh grade team. On top of that, she was a fantastic teacher, and we confided in each other often. She understood the move but was visibly upset as well as were other staff I talked to about a new adventure.

I had set up a time during the day with Coach Phipps to talk to the volleyball and basketball players and let them know I was leaving. Obviously, that was very difficult also, and I figured their reaction would be shocked. This was before the takeoff of social media and cell phones so I don't think they knew what was coming. My meeting was short. I told them I was leaving and thanked them so much for everything they had done for me, and I knew they would find great coaches to replace me. The player reaction when I was done - nothing! No crying, no anger, no questions, nothing! They got up and left and went back to class. I must admit I was quite surprised there wasn't more of a reaction. I'm not sure if they had found out somehow so the shock was off, if they were mad, or if they didn't care. The "no reaction" gave me a feeling at least of maybe from that standpoint, it was the right decision.

When we told my parents, they were supportive but we could definitely tell over the phone that they were disappointed. I think in my whole life, I have always felt a responsibility to not let my parents down in anything that I do, and I definitely felt some of that here. Yes, Margo and I had to do what was best for us, but letting my parents down at this point was very difficult.

Word got out about us going to Mason City, and I was overwhelmed by the responses and how sorry people were that we were leaving. If you remember my first manager in Cherokee, Natasha Olhausen, within hours after it became public, there she was at our door. "Coach, you can't leave; you are staying here!" I explained everything to her and in tears she replied, "Sorry, you aren't going anywhere!" I finally told her that when we got Mason City to the state tournament, I would get her a ticket and she could sit in the front row!

During my time in Mason City, Nana called frequently and once Facebook came out, she would often send me messages. It was always the same questions, "When are you going to state" and "Are you going to buy me a ticket?" When we finally made it to state in 2011, she was one of the first people I contacted and told her I had a ticket for her. Unfortunately, she couldn't make it, but said she would cheer for us from Cherokee.

One of the first people to reach out was Paul Struck, our local newspaper's sports editor. He wrote an all too flattering account of my time in Cherokee (he did claim I said we cried lots of tears over the decision, but that was not true!), and it was clear that I had been able to have some impact on people in Cherokee for which I was very thankful.

Everywhere I have been, I have gained much more from the people I have worked with and been in contact with than I have given to them. One of the positives of working at four different schools has been the opportunity to meet so many fantastic people I have learned so much from at each position. Cherokee is such a great community, and it is because of the people there. Fortunately, with social media, I have been able to stay in contact with many of them over the years even though it has been hard to get back to visit in person.

It then became a whirlwind summer of packing, finding a new place in Mason City, and setting up basketball activities for the summer. Fortunately, we found a buyer for our house fairly quickly at the price we were asking for and settled on a house in Mason City fairly quickly. Our realtor, Abi Lee, was the wife of the football coach and did a great job for us.

I learned one interesting quirk about Mason City while looking at houses with Margo and Abi. North/south streets on one side of town are named after Presidents of the United States and are in the order the Presidents served. On the other end of town, north/south streets are named after states and are in the order that they came into the Union. Pretty cool, but everything was still confusing when we were first looking. I remember being in MC one day to look at houses. Margo and Abi were driving around while I had a meeting, so when I was done, I called and said we could meet somewhere. As I was driving, Abi called and said, "What came first, Carolina or Georgia?" I couldn't remember, but we were eventually able to get things figured out!

I had my first meeting in Mason City, and it went well as 48 kids signed up and everyone seemed excited to get going. I was able to meet two of my assistants, Nicholas Trask and Paul Childress who were ready to get to work. The varsity assistant, Curt Seehusen, decided to not continue coaching, although he continued to be a valued colleague and great friend so we knew we had to hire an assistant to take his place.

I had been asked by my friend Jody Maske to work some of his Chute basketball shooting camps over the years, and the summer of 2007, he had asked me to work some in North Central Iowa. Interestingly enough in June, two of the camps were at Osage and at Central Springs which were very close to Mason City. I ended up working those camps and then had open gyms in Mason City at night. It was definitely a time of no rest for the weary.

I remember at those early, open gyms looking up at the walls and seeing all of the state and conference championships in various sports at Mason City. Conspicuous by its absence was anything for girls' basketball. We made it clear that our goal was to put a banner up there for making the state tournament, and how excited will the community be when that happens! **Simple goal setting is so important in all aspects of life.** I'm not a huge believer in having numerous goals, but having one or two short goals to motivate us every day to get better at what we do is always the way to go. It also gets us through the hard times when things aren't going well and it is easy to get down on life.

Margo and I were able to have all of our possessions moved by a moving company and by the 1st of August, we were officially moved into our house. Much of that time was spent scraping and painting different rooms which turned out to be a very tedious task.

When I started working with the team, I found a group of kids willing to

101

work hard, they were good listeners and had good attitudes. We only had three seniors, and none had played much the year before. Three freshmen had played a lot the year before along with a couple of sophomores. However, there were others ready to step in. We had some good play at team camps, and I felt our kids were very receptive to the up-tempo style we wanted to play.

We also found a varsity assistant. I had a week of new teacher training in August and struck up conversation with a very affable young man named Tom Kirby who was going to be one of our middle school coaches. At an all-district coaches' meeting, I introduced Tom to Coach Trask, and they instantly had a connection. At the end of the night, Coach Trask said, "Why don't we hire that Kirby guy; he's young and inexperienced, but we could teach him!" When I talked to Coach Kirby, he was a bit reluctant but willing to try it. We talked to our new AD Bob Kenny, and he was willing to give that a chance. It was nice to have our staff ready to go even though Coach Trask was the only coach able to help over the summer. A stable staff would prove to be a huge reason for the success that was to come.

Over the 10 years we've been together, Coach Kirby has become an outstanding assistant and trusted friend who has worked incredibly hard for me and for our program. His passion for teaching and for kids is off the charts, and he is always willing to do what is needed for the program. It's interesting to think of how things may have been different if Coach Trask had not suggested that Coach Kirby join us.

Over time, I think I have gotten a lot better at utilizing my assistant coaches, and I wish I could have a do-over with my assistants in my earlier years. I have clearly learned to give them important duties and then get out of their way and trust them to do those duties. I have also learned to give them plenty of say in what we do and although the head coach has to have the final say, feedback and input from assistants is vital. I see too many head coaches today who try to do everything that needs to get done for a program to be successful themselves, and they turn their assistants into glorified statisticians. **Part of the job of head coaches is to add capacity to their assistant coaches.** How does having them sit silently and do stats add to their capacity? **Building trust is vital.** Are assistants going to make poor decisions sometimes? Absolutely! How many bad decisions have I made throughout my career? Thankfully, no one has kept track because the numbers would be huge!

This advice is true for school leaders, business leaders, heads of organizations, and many other groups anyone can think of in the world of work. Getting people to take ownership of responsibilities is good for every organization whether it is in business or school-related. We have tried to do the same thing with our teams. A favorite quote of mine is, "The more the coaches are talking and working, the worse we are. When players take ownership, we are always a lot better." In my opinion, top down leadership is never the way to go.

CHAPTER 16

EYES WIDE OPEN

It's a Tough Road that Leads to the Heights of Greatness

The school year started and for the first time in a long time, I did not have a fall sport to coach. With an all-new teaching curriculum and routine, it was great to be able to work later on classroom activities after school and then head home. I was overwhelmed at times with all of the professional development in MC, but fortunately, I had amazing colleagues who helped keep my head above water and able to keep moving forward.

That fall seemed to take forever, but finally the basketball season was upon us. Practices got off to a great start, and I was optimistic going into our first game at perennial power Ankeny with Hall of Fame coach Scott DeJong. You knew what you were getting with them in tough man-to-man defense, full court press, and patience on offense. We were going to try and press and run them which is the way we wanted to play.

We got off to a good start, but it was clear their pressure was going to bother us. Right before the half, our best post player took a shot to the eye and ended up missing most of the season, which with our lack of size, we couldn't afford. We ended up losing by almost 30 points, something we would have to get used to unfortunately.

We did pull out a win in my first home game in Mason City over Des Moines Hoover by 14 in a ragged game, and then headed to another perennial power West Des Moines Dowling. We again got off to a great start, and it was close early. Unfortunately, their pressure defense completely demoralized us, and I haven't checked official records, but I believe that was the biggest loss differential in my career as we lost 95-28. They continued to press much of the game, and I was fine with that. We needed the practice, but it didn't help. We lost the next two games and then beat Clear Lake in a close game at home to go 2-4 on the season. We hoped to build on the wins and get better as the season went on. Unfortunately, it was our last win of the season.

Our lack of solid ball handling was a major downfall and despite trying numerous players in that spot, including our best player who was a 5'10" wing, it did not get better. It was incredibly frustrating for me and even more so for the players to have other teams dominate us like that. The players kept working hard throughout the season and their attitudes were pretty good, but when you lose that frequently and by those margins, keeping your chin up is very difficult.

One positive was that toward the end of the season, we began to play a 6'2" freshman (to this day, the ONLY 6' or taller player I have ever had!) who had been a very average player in the summer and came on to contribute a bunch at the end of the year. We started her in our tournament game, and she became a huge part of our future success. A question I get asked frequently is, "Do you have any tall players coming up?" It's as if people believe that height is the key to basketball or volleyball. Understand, it would be great to have a plethora of tall athletes at my disposal but that clearly hasn't shown up in my career. I've never believed that height is a direct correlation behind success.

When I was at Atlantic, I remember Coach Jenkins mentioning there was a 6'4" girl in the high school that played tennis. He had been unable to get her out but thought maybe I could. When school started, I actually had her in class and struck up a conversation about tennis. I asked once what she didn't like about tennis. She said, "They make us run around the court, and that's a long ways!" I assumed she wasn't a good fit for me, and I was right. Fortunately, despite having athletes with great height, I have had great numbers of athletes with great desire and work ethic along with great attitude. Give me that any time over someone who only has height. **Skills will also get you a lot farther than height.**

Toward the end of that year, the coaches and I had a couple of discussions with our leading scorer and her parents. They were good conversations, but it was clear they were having issues with some of the things we were doing. I had put a lot of responsibility on this player and at the time, I'm not sure as a sophomore that she was ready for that. However, she was a good kid, and I was looking forward to coaching her for two more years.

After the season ended, I received a call from an opposing coach asking about this player. He had heard that she was transferring to another school. I think coaches are always the last to know with items regarding their players so I kind of brushed it off and said I would check. With AAU basketball becoming a big part of the sport and players from all different towns, they are bound to talk and transfers happen. You don't expect to have to worry about that in Mason City since there aren't bigger towns close to us.

Shortly after that, a fellow coach on staff contacted me and said he was certain she was leaving. He ended up being correct. When I contacted the parents, they admitted the player was transferring to Waukee where my predecessor was now an assistant. It was, they said, mostly for family reasons and more opportunities for the player. It was a shock at first and disappointing as I certainly felt we were moving in the right direction and had some strong classes coming.

I wished them well, and we moved on with plans for the next year. I've always had a pretty good understanding that **if players don't want to be a part of the program, then they should move on to something else and as coaches, we need to move on as well. Worrying about the past and what could have been doesn't get us anywhere. The kids still in the program deserve our time and attention as coaches.**

So, not only had we finished 2-19, but our leading returning scorer was transferring so not the best way to start my Mason City career! Looking back, every first year I have had as a head coach has not been the best record-wise. The second year has always had a better record. I tell first-year head coaches that your first year is always difficult with a new philosophy, more reteaching than ever, kids don't know what to expect, you haven't had time to work with the younger players, and many more issues. Once you've had a year or two under your belt, growth and improvement should be expected.

We moved into year two with confidence that the program would improve. We had an excellent freshman class coming in, and four of them ended up playing significant minutes that year. Our play at the beginning of the year was considerably better than the year before. We were much more competitive with the mid-level teams we played, although the top CIML conference teams we played continued to beat us soundly. We beat archrival Fort Dodge twice in the regular season. Interestingly, we played 23 games that season with only eight at home.

We did not make it through the season without turmoil however. The fact we played four freshmen a lot made many of our upperclassmen and their parents upset. A junior who had started many games the previous two years quit during the season. Another junior, who had played previously also, ran into some issues and did not play varsity that year. Looking back, I should have handled both of those situations better and should have been more patient with both players. I probably didn't communicate well enough with either one.

We ended up 8-15 with a disappointing loss at Fort Dodge in the first round of tournaments. However, we were very pleased with the increase in wins and again had another great group of freshmen coming in to build the program. We were losing four seniors who were fantastic young people with a number who had been part of my initial interview at Mason City. However, we were confident the best was yet to come.

Unfortunately, not everyone felt that way. During that season, I had some discussions with parents who were displeased with parts of the program, particularly the playing time of their daughters. I had been forwarded an email from a parent who expressed deep concerns about my coaching, including comments like "favoritism," "political concerns," and "a comical display of game management." The parent also mentioned he would never "hitch his wagon to this coaching staff." In later years, when I needed some motivation, I pull that email out and remind myself to keep proving people wrong! In case you are wondering, coaches and athletes are always looking for motivation.

I knew things still weren't resolved with some parents but wasn't too concerned about it until I heard from my AD that a group of parents wanted to meet with me. I said that was fine as I have always been open and honest with parents and don't mind discussing things with them. When I arrived at the meeting, it was a full table of mostly junior parents along with my AD Bob Kenny and the high school principal, Doug Kennedy. The meeting turned ugly immediately, and a number of the parents yelled directly at me. One in particular literally screamed at me that all I ever did was yell at his kid (someone who never played and someone I never said anything to!). When I tried to rebuff that, he got even angrier and made some other statements (as did some other parents) against me I would rather not restate here.

I mostly stayed calm and directly answered the questions they had and refuted statements that were made. My statements included saying we would continue to play the best people, the ones we thought deserved to play, and I would continue to coach until Mr. Kenny didn't want me to coach. Finally, Mr. Kennedy announced he had heard enough, that I was his coach, thanks for coming, and the meeting was over.

That was basically the end of that. Most of the players and families that were upset decided to not play any more and that was probably best for everyone. I have been confident in my own abilities, but I was very grateful for the support I received at this time from Bob and Doug. If you coach for any length of time, you are going to have people upset with what you are doing. It simply goes with the territory. If you don't get support from your administration, it isn't worth working for that school. If Doug and Bob had asked me to step aside, I would have done so.

This episode was humbling to go through but was also motivating as I knew we were doing the things needed to succeed, but I also knew people were watching, and if we stopped working, the cynics would be out again. A great work ethic will always keep you advancing in whatever you do, and that is the only way I know how to do things! You also have to believe in what you do. It's fine to listen to what others have to say, but ultimately, we have to stand for something and let the chips fall where they may.

CHAPTER 17

I DID START THE FIRE

Be an Entrepreneur

During the spring of 2009, I had begun to throw around the idea of possibly starting something to help area players develop skills and gain opportunities to improve. AAU basketball was really taking off during that time and unfortunately, North Iowa did not have anything readily available for players. If you wanted that, you needed to travel to Ames, Des Moines, or other farther destinations. A number of our players had played for various AAU programs, and it had helped them improve as players and be seen by college coaches, so I felt something like that was needed in North Iowa.

One day, Margo and I were traveling to Northwest Iowa and the idea hit me to start skills workouts for area players. I gathered some local coaches to help, acquired the use of a couple MC gyms, and set up the skills sessions to begin in the fall. We started with the name the North Iowa Basketball Academy. Response from the area was good, and we had approximately 25 boy and girl athletes who started working with the Academy full-time, and I was pleased with how it progressed. Toward the end of that fall, I had a group of kids and their parents approach me to ask if there was any way we would continue into the spring and summer and start up AAU teams that could travel to various tournaments, get better, and get exposure to college coaches.

I must admit that I hadn't thought much about that previously and figured athletes in North Iowa (many who were three and four sport athletes) would be more concerned about the skills part. So, we decided to put something together for the spring of 2010. After much digging on the Internet trying to find the right name, we decided on the North Iowa Fire. So when people ask, I have to disagree with Billy Joel's hit song; I really did start the Fire!

Because we didn't have full rosters that first year, we ended up combining age divisions so our first teams were quite raw. I was able to get former NIACC women's coach John Oertel as well as Coach Kirby to help coach the teams. One of our first tournaments was down in Ames against teams that had played together for many years and had some of the region's best athletes. You can guess the results. We were crushed in many of the games and even laughed at by opposing teams.

The message from me was always the same to the athletes. **You are playing great competition, and if you keep working hard, learn from your mistakes, and keep a great attitude, it will pay off in the long run, and you will get better.** You won't remember the scores of these games once you wake up tomorrow. As the years have passed, our Fire teams have gotten progressively better and today can compete with most of the programs in the region. At one point, we had over 200 athletes from 25 area schools playing with us.

One of the joys of working with the Fire has been seeing these local athletes improve and shine once they get to high school, becoming mainstays for their local programs. We are now at the point that many of our Fire players move on to playing at the college level and end up receiving college scholarships because of their play. It's very gratifying to read the local paper during our season and be able to name all of the Fire players who led their teams to victory and in some statistical category.

Today, I am not as directly involved with the Fire as the time commitment especially for the weekend tournaments has become more difficult. Fortunately, we have built a great partnership with NIACC, the community college in Mason City, and their head women's basketball coach, Todd Ciochetto, has done a great job with the girls' side. We also added a boys' side a few years ago and hope to continue to build opportunities for athletes in North Iowa.

Another life changing event for me started in 2009. When we were still in Cherokee, I had looked at getting my master's degree, but hadn't found the right situation for me. The last year we were there, Drake had sent out information about an educational leadership program they were hosting, and I was intrigued. It would involve a lot of weekends for two years, and I would drive to Denison an hour away for the classes. I talked to the person heading it up, Dr. Bill Wright, a former superintendent at Denison, and I was impressed with his passion and personality. I was considering signing up in the spring of 2007, but then the Mason City job came up, and it all fell through.

Fast-forward to the fall of 2008, and I received information that Drake was offering the same master's program as a cohort in Mason City on the NIACC campus, starting in late January of 2009. What a deal. I would only have to drive 10 minutes to class and could work with others from the area. It was going to be a lot of work and a lot of time (Saturday's 8:30-4:30 and Sunday's 8:30-1:30), but having a master's gives you a large pay bump, and the educational leadership program allows you to be a K-12 principal as well. It's not like I've ever had a yearning to be a principal, but this would give me options going forward, and I hoped it would be a great learning experience as well.

The first class was set up for the last weekend of January, 2009. We had our highly successful Coaches vs. Cancer game vs. Marshalltown the Friday night before so there was a lot going on. I was quite nervous about the start of it as well. I didn't know what to expect, how was I going to handle all of the weekends in class, would it be meaningful to my life, etc.

Then earlier in the week before the first class, we received an email from a close Cherokee friend. Ken Lee, our next-door neighbor in Cherokee and our driver during our wedding day, had died suddenly of an aneurysm. The visitation was Friday night and the funeral Saturday morning. What a blow it was to lose Ken, and the services were at difficult times for us. I knew Friday night was out because of the game, and Saturday was my first day of class and felt I couldn't miss. I talked to my Drake advisor, Dr. Jan Walker, and she couldn't have been nicer about it. As she would say numerous times during my two years of classes, "Do what is best for your situation; if you have to miss, it is not a problem." Those words were reassuring, but I also hated missing the initial class where so much of the relationship building in the cohort would begin. There were twelve people total enrolled, and I wanted to get off to a good start with everyone.

I honestly had a couple of sleepless nights about what to do. I needed to do both and yet could only pick one. I finally decided to stay and go to class and have regretted it ever since. The fact I wasn't there to support Ken's wife Molly and family is still disappointing even though she was very good about it when I talked to her. Even during that first class, I couldn't get what was going on in Cherokee out of my mind. Since then, I have always tried to error on the human side when having tough decisions to make, but that doesn't make it any easier.

Overall, getting my master's through Drake was a fantastic experience. My cohort included three colleagues from my middle school which made it easier. The professors were terrific, and one of the best happened to be Bill Wright formerly from Denison. We ended up with two classes with Bill, and they were both fantastic. There were so many positives about Bill as an instructor. He was a great storyteller, which always kept things interesting. He asked great questions and made sure everyone was able to give their side. Plus, his passion for teaching and his students was unmatched. He mentioned that he and some colleagues were writing a book about his four P's: People, Passion, Purpose, and Perseverance. It was inspiring to hear him talk about these ideas, and it has made me a better educator, and I believe a better person.

Bill actually inspired me to start the idea of the North Iowa Fire, and to this day, remains a mentor when I have questions and need to bounce ideas off someone. He is now retired and living the good life in San Diego where his wife is one of the top rowing coaches in the country. **All of us need a mentor like this in someone who challenges our thinking but also inspires us to make an impact on the lives of others.** This inspiration created one of his favorite phrases, the "ripple effect" and having an impact on many others down the road.

During the two years of my master's program, I was able to experience a number of great educational experiences through working with our cohort and working with various administrators which gave me a chance to experience situations that principals might face. One day, I was covering the afternoon for the high school principal who had a meeting at Central Office, so I was totally "in charge" for the afternoon. The principal told me to walk around and observe classrooms if I wanted and spend the end of the afternoon in his office. I was given his "walkie talkie" in case something happened, but the afternoon was very quiet so about 3:00, I went back to his office and checked my email on the computer.

Suddenly, I heard on the walkie-talkie, "There's smoke coming out of the upstairs boys' bathroom!" By the time I stood up, the fire alarms were going off! I ran out and asked the secretary where that was and then sprinted to that spot. When I got upstairs, there was a lot of smoke pouring out of there! Students and teachers were great and were getting out of the building quickly and quietly. I walked into the bathroom and a custodian who was a sub for the day was walking toward a garbage can that was on fire. When I asked what he was doing, he said, "I'm going to carry the garbage can outside." Obviously, that was not a good idea! I told him to wait and asked where the fire extinguisher was, and he indicated right outside the door. I yelled, "Grab the fire extinguisher and put the fire out!" The custodian proceeded to do that, and the fire was fortunately put out quickly. We closed the bathroom door and went back out to make sure students were out of the building and to make sure the fire department knew where we were.

After the fire department arrived and made sure everything was clear, I headed back to the office to see what else needed to be done. The principal happened to be coming in at that time and started laughing loudly when he saw me. I believe my comment was, "This was the first and only time I will cover for you!" Fortunately, no one was hurt and no property was damaged. All of the staff was very professional and was well trained as to how to handle an emergency like that. I was lucky to have knowledgeable people around to help me get through something I would have never imagined would happen!

Since I have earned my masters degree, I have given thought to moving into administration but have never taken the plunge. It is mostly because I would have to give up coaching and there wasn't much pay difference (sometimes I would have received less) so it has been an easy decision. I have continued to build my leadership capacity and help out where needed. **Leadership doesn't just have to come from the top of the leadership chain. It can come from everyone.** I have had a lot of positive things happen in my professional life since 2009, and I truly feel my master's program and working with people like Bill Wright, certainly has helped make many of these things happen. **It goes to show the importance of education, and particularly educators on all of**

those young people in the educational system.

2009 was also a year of health concerns for my lovely bride. You may be wondering why at this point there has not been a mention of children in our family. Obviously, we both married later in life (I was 36 at the time) so although we had talked about having kids possibly, we weren't sure. Margo had also been diagnosed with endometriosis, which is a very painful disorder that creates cysts in the uterus that spreads to other areas. She had minor surgery in Cherokee but continued to have a lot of issues with that, and it makes having children almost impossible. When we got to Mason City and she saw a doctor here, he called it one of the worst cases of endometriosis he had ever seen.

Margo had always had a lot of pain with it and also had severe migraines from time to time which the endometriosis was probably making worse as well. She continued to take medications but continued to have issues with it. In September of 2009, it all came to a boil. We had talked about what the best steps were going forward and had finally decided that a hysterectomy was the best way to go and help her become pain-free. It meant no kids, but we were both OK with that. I had plenty of kids in my life, and she was an only child and didn't want a child to experience that. We talked to the doctor and he concurred. The surgery was set up for October.

One day in late September, I had headed off to school, and I knew Margo was in quite a bit of pain. She eventually called to say the pain was unbearable so I headed home, and we called her mom as well. We agreed we needed to get her to the doctor. As we waited in the room for the doctor, she literally curled up in a ball because of all the pain. When her doctor came in, he said it would be best to have the hysterectomy immediately to make sure nothing else was going on. He was not available until the next morning so we decided to get her admitted to the hospital and have the surgery the next morning.

Although the time before surgery was off the charts painful for Margo, the surgery itself went well, and all of the reports came back negative, so we were very thankful. They did show us pictures of the area that was removed and it was obvious why she had so much pain. We were thankful to have that over, and Margo's health has been much improved since then. Neither of us has had any regrets on not having any kids of our own and are thankful for good health.

I haven't talked much about my wife in here and that is the way she wants it. She has never enjoyed the spotlight and would rather stay out of the way and not be the center of attention. However, I am so blessed to have her in my life. She has given me balance and a much better perspective on life overall. It's no secret that my coaching career has been much more successful since we were married. Why is that? As I mentioned earlier, we don't talk about the games when we get home. We watch TV, talk about other things, or worry about our cat. Margo is also the most honest person I have ever met and will tell me exactly what she thinks. We ALL need that person in our life, especially the more successful we become. **If you surround yourself with "yes" people, you will always think you are right when admitting mistakes and learning from them are a great way for us to grow.**

Like every marriage, we have had our ups and downs, and it is always a work in progress. However, having Margo by my side for my biggest achievements has enhanced the effects greatly and has put everything in perspective for me. What a lucky man I am! Enough on Margo before she throws something at me for talking about her too much!

I can't go on before I talk about someone who has been a part of the family for our entire marriage, and in fact has been with Margo longer than I have - our cat, Posy! Unfortunately, Posy passed away as I finished this book. I always say she has been spoiled beyond belief and that is the reason for the longevity! She had a privileged life and has only left the house for trips to the veterinarian and when we moved.

It's hard to describe the impact that Posy had on our lives. Until recently, she usually started my day as she seemed to have an inner sense of when I was supposed to get up in the morning. Posy would jump up on our bed and meow in my face as if to say, "Get up, it's time for school!" She would then follow me into the bathroom as I got ready and then made sure to try and jump up on my lap when I sat down to eat breakfast. When I got home from school, there was Posy wondering where I had been and ready to make sure she was taken care of.

Although Posy has tested our patience over the years, her energy, loyalty, and stability have greatly added to our lives and although she wasn't a human, we have almost treated her as one. We treat her as an important part of our lives and our worlds changed greatly when she passed.

After an eventful 2009, year three of basketball saw more changes to our roster as three more freshmen came in and contributed immediately to our team. Combining those three with our returners gave us the confidence that we were good enough to compete with anyone in the conference. We continued to add players with AAU experience who played year round with other players from our conference so there was no reason to fear any opponents we faced.

Although we started with a tough loss to highly ranked Des Moines East, we proceeded to win our next five games, including wins over SE Polk and Valley, who had handled us easily in previous years. Two tough losses to Johnston and Waukee followed, but we roared out of the holiday break with six more wins in a row, an 11-3 record, and our first ever ranking.

Unfortunately, the rest of the season was more difficult as a very tough schedule was hard to overcome. Ankeny beat us by three at home and our nemesis Waukee beat us badly at home as well. We lost our last two regular season games, a difficult one-point loss at home to Dowling, and we were blown out by 30 at Ames. That was an interesting game as we knew we would open tournament play a week later at home with them again. I purposely held back some of the suggestions we would have done so that we had some tricks for them in the tournament. Some of the players weren't thrilled with that, and I understood, but the head coach always has to have the big picture in mind, and the big picture was the tournament game. We had not won a tournament game since I had arrived, and it was at home, so we liked our chances.

However, we got off to a slow start and trailed 15-2 after a quarter and 23-18 at the half. We only gave up 16 points the last three quarters, but unfortunately, could only score 27 ourselves the last three quarters and ended up losing 31-29. They made two free throws with 50 seconds left (another questionable call...those darn officials!), and we had a wide-open three-footer roll off the rim with three seconds left. We failed to score the last 4:50 of the game despite great shots. It was a very disappointing way to end the season, but what progress we had made! We finished 13-8 and 7-3 in the conference, the best records in a long time. At the end of the Ames game, we had three freshmen, a sophomore, and a junior on the floor. The good news was that as we put on our end of the season booklet "The Best is Yet to Come!"

CHAPTER 18

AN HISTORIC SEASON
Reaching for the Top

The 2010-11 season came with high expectations. We started the season ranked ninth, our first ever preseason ranking. However, as I reminded the players, ninth would not be high enough to make it to state as only eight teams make it. However, we all knew that the goal was to put the first ever state banner on the wall. We started the season with an exhibition game with Mason City Newman called the Hall of Pride Game. It was not an official game, but it ended up to be a fundraiser for our local United Way, which helps so many people in the area. We ended up winning the game by a huge margin (we definitely didn't run up the score), and a lot of money was raised. Since then, we have started every year with the Hall of Pride activities that have helped the United Way and Crisis Intervention Services. We have also built a huge Coaches vs. Cancer Fundraiser in January every year that has become one of the state's biggest and best. I am incredibly proud of the numerous activities our players do to give back to the community. It is vital they understand the value of service to their communities and is something we all can do more of to help in the area. **Sports are an important part of the girls' lives, but when sports end for them, they need to know and be thinking about the bigger picture.**

We started the season with a huge win over Clear Lake which led to game two at home vs. #1 ranked Des Moines East. They had five future Division I players on that team and were very intimidating. Many of our players had played AAU ball with and against them so there was a bit of a fear factor. Before the game, we had talked about the importance of playing our game of running and pressing and to see what happened. When the game tipped off, it was clear something was not right. Our players only played a token press and truly never got after East full-court like we wanted. It was as if they had chosen to play differently than what I wanted. Despite my urgings, nothing changed, and the game was never really close. We lost by 17, and it could have been worse.

My assistants and I had believed the players had made their own decision to play a different style so the next day at practice, we pulled the captains aside, and that was indeed the case. They did not think they were good enough to run and press with a team like East. Wow! I didn't know how to respond. I expressed my disappointment in their decision and that I wouldn't do anything more about it at the time. We let them know that if it happened again, they would be removed from the game and would sit next to us. The rest of the season, there were no issues, but looking back, I wish I would have handled it differently during the game. My thought at the time was to not mess up the game by becoming angry at the players, but waiting made it worse and obviously sent the wrong message to the team. Coaches have to make thousands of decisions during a season with little time to think about it, and I clearly have made my share of errors.

When I think back to my career, I think too many times I did not take care of situations that arose right at the time and instead hoped that patience and staying calm were the way to go. Most of the time that might work, but when it comes to game situations, issues should be cleared up immediately. I think it hurt my standing with this group in the future as it may have made the players believe I wasn't as decisive as I needed to be. As a coach and as a human being, **we will always make mistakes. We need to just learn from them and try not to repeat them in the future. I think admitting you have messed up is also vital.** Denying wrongdoing definitely doesn't help anyone and instead makes it last longer than necessary.

After the East game, we won our next three games fairly easy heading into a showdown with archrival Waukee, a team we had never beaten. It was a crazy game with a lot of back and forth that finally led to overtime. We took the lead late, but they hit a shot with a few seconds left to win 70-69. It was a bitter loss but more evidence that our team was growing into a state tournament type team. We rebounded with six straight wins leading to a rematch with Waukee at home. Would this be the time we finally defeated them? Not this time. Our best defender went out early in the week with appendix surgery, and they jumped on us 19-3 after a quarter. Despite outscoring them the rest of the way, we lost by 12, another disappointing loss to Waukee.

A win over Ames followed, and we then headed to #2 Ankeny, another team we had failed to defeat in my time in Mason City. With a balanced attack and great pride, we went on the attack and beat them 48-45, probably the biggest win our program had since I arrived. It again showed that we could beat anyone in the state on any floor.

We went on a seven-game winning streak at that point, including a 28-point win over Cedar Falls. We knew they would be hosting in the first round of tournaments. However, things were still not perfect as the coaches and I ended up having a meeting with a couple players and their parents before and after the Cedar Falls game because of some other things that had come up where the players weren't following the standards we expected. The timing wasn't great, but we felt with the air cleared, we could keep things together for the rest of the season.

Team confidence was sky-high going into the last two regular season games at Valley and Dowling, two tough tests, but we knew those would make us better for the tough tournament trail. The Valley game started and remained close throughout, and we in fact led into the third quarter when suddenly our starting point guard and leading scorer went down in a heap with an ankle injury. Oh no! Immediately the rest of the season flashed before all of our eyes. She ended up having some torn ligaments, but trainers were hopeful she might be able to get back sometime during tournaments. Unfortunately, we fell apart without her and lost to Valley by 11. We then played a makeup game with Dowling a few days later and lost also by 11.

We had four days to prepare for our first tournament game with Cedar Falls with a lot of unknowns. We didn't know if our point guard would play, and we had lost our last two games. We also still had never won a tournament game, but at least we would be at home. Cedar Falls also had a record of only 4-18 but also had a lot of tall, athletic kids, which usually gave us trouble. Despite struggling most of the game and never being able to pull away, we found a way to win, 51-46. They were much more aggressive than us and hit more shots than game one. Fortunately, one of our freshmen stepped up with 20 points, and we held on. We had all the pressure on us for that game and knew we would be the underdog as we moved on to the regional final against #4 Waterloo West.

West was a talented, experienced team led by Hall of Fame coach Dr. Tony Pappas, who was a Mason City native and grew up about a block from my house in Mason City. In fact, my wife and I would see Tony's brother and mom a lot, especially on the walking track by our house. One of his assistants was Gary Sinnwell, a former Mohawk girls' basketball coach so I knew the game meant a lot to them.

The big question was whether our point guard would be able to play. She hadn't practiced since she was injured but had done a lot of rehab. Even if she was cleared to play, we didn't know what she would be able to give. She was a real gamer though and very tough so we knew we would get everything she had. About 2:00 the afternoon of the game, I received a note that her trainer and doctor had cleared her to play, which was a great boost of confidence. We certainly played up the underdog role and felt confident going in.

The game was played in Clarksville (we did take a bus, not a train if you get that reference!), a much smaller town between Waterloo and Mason City. They had a fairly new gym although it was much smaller than what either of us had played in before. It didn't really bother me as it was the same for both teams. We weren't sure exactly how long it would take to get there, and of course, we arrived really early. I like to get to away games an hour or so ahead of the game, and we were there probably and hour and a half ahead of time. I think the sitting around made our kids more nervous, however. The nerves showed at the beginning as we got behind early and trailed by six at the end of one and the half. We didn't start our point guard but got her in, and she was obviously not herself and quite rusty. The third quarter wasn't much better as we couldn't buy a basket, especially from the three-point arc.

Going into the fourth quarter, we were down eight, and West quickly bumped it to ten. One of our best defenders hit her head and had to come out for a stretch so we were even more shorthanded. Players were starting to hang their heads, and we just kept coming back to one of our old mottos...you gotta play 32 minutes. Finally, our press started to have more effect, and we slowly cut the deficit. They also started missing some key free throws (2 of 12 in the last quarter) which got us close. We were down four with forty seconds left and our point guard, who somehow found a burst of energy in the fourth quarter, hit a big three to cut it to one. We had to foul with 25 seconds left, but they missed both shots! Unfortunately, we turned it over and had to foul again, but they amazingly missed two more free throws. We had one more chance!

We did not call time out as our philosophy is to keep the momentum going and only call time out if we are out of whack. We called our simple "fist" play, basically a high screen for our point guard. She dribbled off the screen, drove baseline, went up, got knocked down (the video is clear) and....the officials called a foul. I finally got a call late in a tournament game.

Our point guard went to the line, down one, three seconds left, state tournament berth on the line, and calmly swished the first one! She shot the second and knocked it down! (She went on to play Division I basketball). We were up by one! We called timeout to set the defense and make sure we didn't foul and kept them in front of us. They threw the ball in. Our defender got caught and their player had a free lane down the floor. She got just outside the arc and launched a shot that looked good from my angle. The shot missed, and we were headed to state for the first time ever at Mason City for girls' basketball! The score was 33-32. The game was very similar to my first regional final win at Cherokee with lots of nerves, lots of missed shots, close game, players making some clutch plays at the end, and some luck involved.

As you can imagine, pandemonium ensued as the coaches had a large group hug. I believe Coach Kirby jumped into my arms first! We went to shake hands with the Waterloo coaches, and I truly felt bad for Coach Pappas and Coach Sinnwell. They were incredibly gracious considering the toughness of the loss. They both came over again long after the game to express how happy they were for us. I couldn't have had more respect for them after that and to this day, we continue to keep in contact and scrimmage them every Christmas break in Waterloo. By the time we got to the locker room, our point guard was literally curled up in a corner because her ankle was so sore. What a performance under pressure, but it showed how far she was away from being 100% healthy.

First state team at Mason City in 2011

One of the first calls I received in congratulations was from Dan Delaney, the Athletic Director who hired me. He was so thrilled, and in fact started crying over the phone. He lived in Minneapolis at this time but expressed how proud he was to be a Mohawk and offered to buy the team a meal in Des Moines! I received a number of congratulations after that (over 100 emails, I believe!), and it was almost overwhelming! It goes to show something that we talk to teams about all the time. **Your actions (especially as an athlete) have a large impact on many people, and many times on people we have no idea about.** The community support was off the charts, and so many people let me know how it had impacted them. That is one of the payoffs of working so hard at what we do. My only regret was that the previous years of players at MC never had a chance to experience the thrill of making it to state. It shows also that state appearances are not easy, and you need skill but also some luck and breaks to go your way at times.

We found out we were to play SE Polk the first game at state. We had played them in the CIML Jamboree at the beginning of the year but did not play them during the regular season. We were hoping to get our point guard healthier and tried to keep the team's focus on giving a great performance. We did get off to a good start and led 12-7 after one quarter. However, we hit a real dry spell in the second quarter and ended up trailing by four at the half. Another slow quarter in the third put us down ten and despite a lot of fight, we lost 49-35. We ended up 1-15 from the three-point arc and even our best free throw shooters struggled. We were 5-17 from the line in the first half alone and 10-23 for the game. I also felt like I needed to mix up our defenses more, and I had put our injured point guard on their all-conference point guard. Normally, it would have been a great matchup for us, but the injury obviously slowed her down. I'm not sure that tactical error was the reason we lost, but it didn't help matters.

Our 6'2" girl played a great game in her last appearance as a Mohawk with 11 points, eight rebounds, and seven blocked shots, but we just couldn't get her the ball more. She went on to have an excellent volleyball career at Northern Iowa and what a place to end her outstanding sports career.

It was not the way we wanted things to end, but it was truly a history-making season. How in the world did we get to the point of success we did after starting 2-19? 1. Our players worked extremely hard on their own and became better players. 2. Players bought in and played as a team. They got along great. 3. We had great support from administration and the community. 4. The assistant coaches were passionate about the game and were great teachers both in and out of the classroom.

Continuity on staff played a big part in the success we had. Coach Kirby has been my varsity assistant ever since we met at new teacher training and has grown into the position and into a vital part of the team, including taking over our huge Coaches vs. Cancer initiative and being in charge of post play and out of bounds plays. Coach Nick Trask was a huge part of our program for seven years as the JV coach and in charge of the defense before moving on to the head boys' basketball position at MC. Coach Childress was our freshmen coach for three years before stepping aside for Coach Katie Trask who has been with us for the last six years. Interestingly, we made state her first year and five of her first six years are a credit to her passion and knowledge of the game along with terrific teaching abilities. Later, we added Coach Britney Borchardt after Coach Nick Trask moved on, and she has continued our strong tradition of having great teachers and role models for our athletes.

In today's sports' world, even at the high school level, there is a mad rush to expect winning immediately and a rush to get rid of coaches that don't succeed immediately. We are in a society of "instant gratification" so to speak, and I'm thankful that despite my starting new jobs with poor records, administrators have believed in me and given me time to work with my coaches and build a program, not just have a great season. That means working with youth teams which takes time to see the end result. I have been very lucky to have amazing assistant coaches who care about kids and give back to them and myself as a head coach as much as they do. Having that "team" around me makes my job so much easier.

Unfortunately, in April of 2011, our family faced another medical crisis, this time with Mom. She had always been the family caretaker, especially with Dad's issues. Other than her pacemaker, Mom's health had been good, although she had some minor issues and her doctor decided in January a colonoscopy would be good considering she had never had one, and my grandfather had died of colon cancer at age 70. Doctors found a polyp that they didn't like and decided to have another colonoscopy done in April. This showed that things were getting worse.

Despite Mom wanting to wait with surgery because of having to take care of Dad, doctors pushed for surgery as soon as possible. Mom reluctantly relented and after checkups with her heart and eye doctors (needed because of her previous issues), surgery was set up immediately for April 26th, which was also Dad's 82nd birthday. My family was reluctant of that date because of his birthday and the issues that could come up, but I finally said, "Everything could work out great as well and what an awesome birthday present that would be!"

Mom's big worry (always thinking of others) was who would take care of Dad's urine bag as that would need to be taken care of, cleaned, and changed occasionally. Fortunately, a wound specialist nurse at the Sanford Hospital would do it and just called it "checking up on things." This made all of us feel better, and we offered to pitch in where needed as well. I decided to take the week off from school, and Dad and I stayed at my brother Larry and sister-in-law Mary Jane's place in Sioux Falls which was very convenient.

Not surprisingly, Mom kept an amazingly positive attitude before surgery and continued to be worried about everyone else and not herself. Surgery was very long and complicated but after it was done, the doctors came out and said everything went very well. The polyp was removed, and it had cancer cells but fortunately they were contained. Every test they took to see if any cancer cells had escaped to other parts were negative. PRAISE THE LORD!!

Mom was very groggy 12 hours after the surgery, but as Dad and I were sitting bedside, here came the nurses, "OK, Kathryn, it's time for you to get up and walk!" The look on Mom's face was priceless, and I think Dad's was similar! I had to reassure Dad that they needed to get her system moving to get her back to normal. She was walking more the next day in the hall and farther every time.

Three days later, all of the tests came back negative, which meant NO CHEMO WAS NEEDED and the doctor said in another day or two they could dismiss her. Mom was on no pain pills and all tubes were removed, and she went home in five days. She has had blood work and CT-scans every year for five years and all have been negative. PRAISE THE LORD!

It's just another reason why our Coaches vs. Cancer event is so important to me. Cancer has affected all of us in so many ways and without the research and work that has been done to this point, undoubtedly, neither of my parents would have had much of a chance to survive. We all owe it to future generations to do everything we can to rid the world of this awful disease.

CHAPTER 19

DISAPPOINTMENT CAN LEAD TO SUCCESS

You Can't Always Get What you Want

Although the previous year ended in disappointment, hopes were again high for the 2011-2012 season as we had six players returning who were key cogs in the previous year's great run. The state felt the same way and ranked us at #3 to start the season. We felt like we had a team that could compete for a state title, but one forgotten item was that we had not won a conference title yet. The conference was reconfigured a bit so it was a bit tougher to win, and we also had ten conference games now.

We won our first four games including a big win at Des Moines East a team we had not beaten since I had arrived in Mason City. That led to a match up with Waukee on the road. In a trend that would continue until the last game, it was another odd game with them. Our point guard re-injured her ankle during the game, and we struggled to score late. We did take a lead late in the game, but they hit a shot on a putback with four seconds left to win by two. I found out later that was the 11th straight loss to Waukee and many in frustrating fashion. There would be more to come with Waukee. We rolled through our next seven games and our point guard came back to finish the season strong. This led to a rematch with who else, Waukee at home.

A quick back-story...during this time, I had applied to the district for a new data team position and received two interviews. I hadn't heard anything and was starting to forget about it. At 3:30 on the day of the game, my superintendent called to say they had hired someone else. I was really disappointed at the time and for some reason became very fired up. I'm not sure if it was losing out for this new position or the timing or the fact that we were playing Waukee, but I was very emotional. I would say that game might have been the most fired up I have been throughout a whole game in my career. I'm sure the losing to Waukee 11 straight times, losing a player to them, then losing out on a job, made it a combination of things. Fortunately, our players took care of things for me, and we played one of our best games of the season to win 63-53 in a game that wasn't that close. remember telling the media that it doesn't get much better than this, which was a slight bit of hyperbole, but it was definitely enjoyable!

We had to turn around and host #2 Ankeny. Suddenly, a conference title was a possibility with our first loss to Waukee being a "non conference" game because of conference rules. Despite a huge height advantage, we took down Ankeny and found ourselves leading the conference. We continued on with an 11-game winning streak heading into another big game at home with Dowling. Our hot streak ended as their height and strength were too much, and they undoubtedly played their best game of the season. We were very disappointed but knew there was still a lot to play for.

Everything broke right for us and going to the next to the last conference game at Fort Dodge, we knew that if we won, we would be the outright conference champions. We talked to our booster reps and Decker's Sporting Goods rep Al Koehler ahead of time and had a shirt made proclaiming us conference champs. Now, those who know me know I am VERY humble when it comes to these things and also do not want to put the proverbial "cart before the horse" so to speak. However, we felt confident we would get the win, and our kids deserved the credit. We ended up winning by 34, wrapping up the first ever CIML Conference Title. Needless to say, it was a joyous locker room, made even more special by the shirts for everyone!

It goes back to something I've always believed with teaching and coaching from an early age in that **you have to celebrate the little things and have fun with what you are doing. A key to successful teams, businesses, schools, etc. is a team mindset and a team that works hard together but has fun together. If you fail to celebrate successes, it can ultimately hurt your bottom line and drive people from either staying with you or at least working to get better.** My teams have always celebrated the little things, and we will continue to do so.

We ended the regular season at 19-2, 9-1 in the conference, and ranked third. We were very confident going into tournaments and had a good road to state we felt. The best CIML teams were in other regions and the state sent us west so a regional final would be with Sioux City West, a team that did not play a schedule like we did.

We opened tournaments with Boone, and I knew if this was a game, it was all on us. We literally played a perfect first half leading 23-3 after one quarter and 53-14 at the half. All 15 of our players played in the first half and one of our freshmen hit a buzzer beater going into halftime. We continued to roll 87-28, hitting a school record sixteen 3-pointers!

Our regional final was against SC West in Fort Dodge and from watching tapes, we knew it was going to be an interesting game. They were very scrappy, very aggressive, and at times, very foul prone, but we were confident our press would give them fits. We had a very interesting pre-game that I didn't find out about until after the game. For some reason, Fort Dodge put their student section (very small but VERY vocal) right behind our bench. Apparently, they were saying nasty things to our players and some threats even came out. My assistants tried to ask the FD administration to move the fans and instead got in trouble with FD and then with our AD about the request. They didn't want me to worry about it, but clearly that is something I should have known about. West probably had no more than 100 people at the game, while we had almost an entire side filled. Our crowd support, especially our student section, has been amazing during my time at MC!

Fortunately, our players put the distractions to the side and played a great game jumping out early 19-8 and then running away at the half 49-15. As the game continued, we felt like some of our players were getting cheap-shotted, and we began to worry about injuries. We ended up rolling on to state 76-48, and our confidence was at an all-time high. We weren't intimidated by the state surroundings and knew we were as good as anyone in the state.

Who would we play at state? Of course, Waukee! It would be the rubber game since we had each won a game during the regular season. There wouldn't be any surprises and whoever played the best that day would win the game. We had a great week of practice leading up to the game and felt good about our chances. We controlled the first half and led by nine. Unfortunately, the second half was a defensive nightmare. We did not play as well as we could have, and I did not make enough adjustments to help our team out. They shot 93% in the second half. Yes, 93%! They took 13 shots from two-point range in the half, and made every shot. They just couldn't miss in the second half of the game.

Despite that, we fought back from a tie at the end of the third quarter to lead by five midway through the fourth quarter. All we needed was to keep the momentum on our side, and we just couldn't get it. Despite that, the game was tied with under a minute left, and we had the ball. Like usual, I decided to not call timeout and let our kids play. Our point guard had an opening, may have been bumped, and was called for traveling with around 10 seconds left. On the final possession, Waukee brought the ball down the court. One of their players dribbled along the sideline, appeared to travel by taking extra steps (the video showed this), and proceeded to knock down a shot as the clock ran out. Our season ended at the buzzer and Waukee stuck another dagger in our hearts.

Yes, it appeared the officials missed an obvious travel, but the hard facts were that they shot 93%, and we did not make needed adjustments. This was a hard loss to recover from as it's easy to second-guess yourself as a coach after a game like that. Why didn't I change up defenses more? Should we have called more timeouts? Would a different lineup have helped? Our players took it hard as well and had a tough time getting through the media interviews after the game. It was great to see players take accountability for losing, but it was not their fault. We would have never gotten as far as we did without their great efforts and commitment to the team.

The 2012-13 season brought about continued high expectations. Our seniors had led the team with amazing success and were hungry to get back to state and make an impact. We had another freshman coming in ready to make a big impact. As in previous years, we were given a high preseason ranking at #2 and won our first two games easily. The #1 ranked team lost so we moved up to the #1 spot which was a great honor for a program that had come so far. We knew it might not last, and it didn't. We had been invited to play in a prestigious tournament in Minneapolis and played perennial power Bloomington Kennedy. They ended up beating us in a close game, but it was great to be challenged by one of the best teams in another state and proved that we belonged with the best.

The 2012-13 school year started with an unforgettable tragedy. Royal Wentworth taught 8th grade social studies with me at the middle school and was an all around great teacher and human being. At our beginning of the year meeting in 2012, I sat by Royal and we talked for probably a half hour. He talked so much about his love of teaching and his love of his wife and daughters. When you met Royal, you were immediately taken back by his deep, booming voice, and his friendly, outgoing demeanor. Everyone loved Royal!

On September 10th, Royal was out doing two things he loved: running and being with students. He was running with his middle school cross country team when he collapsed and died of a heart attack. It was a tragic loss as Royal was a revered member of not only the school but the community. It was a difficult time for the staff and students at the middle school as Royal was beloved by everyone. The visitation was packed and we waited over an hour and a half to see the family. The funeral was packed as well. It was another example of how fragile life is and how important it is to live your life to the fullest and treat people the right way.

We bounced back three days later to win at SE Polk as one of our freshmen broke out with a huge game of 18 points and four 3-pointers. We rolled through the next nine games, returning to the #1 spot in the state, and entered a huge game against #2 Ankeny. It was our annual Coaches vs. Cancer game and the entire gym was full. People were kept from entering by local officials because of gym capacity being reached. What a credit to our kids for building the program to that level!

Unfortunately, as we came into the game our point guard had injured her ankle for the third straight year and missed a number of games, including that one. Our next point guard, our best three-point shooter, injured her ankle in the third quarter, further putting us at disadvantage. Despite that, we were in control going into the fourth quarter, but Ankeny made a run to send it to overtime tied at 32. We took the lead in overtime, but they hit a bucket with three seconds left to win the game. It was a tough loss considering the injuries but showed the true grit the team had. Our biggest concern became getting everyone healthy. We decided to take a cautionary approach and not bring both players back until they were cleared as 100% healthy. We proceeded to win our next three games without them, and they were both cleared by the trainers to play in our next game at Ames but only for very short spurts.

The game started, and we followed the game plan. Both players said they felt good and wanted to stay in. However, we stuck with the long-term game plan, and it affected the overall play of the team. There was a lot of "discussion" with them about winning the game and letting them play more. I knew keeping them out there was best to help us win that game, but I felt the long-term prognosis, and especially following what the trainer had told us was best for business. They disagreed and let those feelings be known. Unfortunately, it was all downhill from there, and we lost by 17. Ames was good but not 17 points better. I loved the competitiveness of the players but could not convince them why this was the right call. Looking back, I let it go on too long and wasn't tough enough in letting them know that this is what they needed to believe in and to get on board or get off. This issue would come back to affect us later on in the season.

With both players back healthy, we ran through the last four regular season games, including a huge win at Dowling by six. That gave us a tie for the top of the overall CIML Conference Title for the second year in a row, and we had won the conference. We felt we were the best team in the state and just needed to prove it. We started tournaments with a fairly easy win over Cedar Falls at home and moved on the regional final for the third year in a row. Our opponent was Dubuque Senior, a team with an 11-11 record and one that had not played the schedule we had played. Everyone expected an easy game.

Unfortunately, that was not the case. They jumped on us early, leading by nine at one point and by five at halftime. We had two starters in foul trouble, and they were much more aggressive. Obviously, no one was happy, particularly me. We had not gotten after it defensively at all and played quite passively. I talked to the team about pressing the second half and a couple of our captains responded with, "We don't need to press; we'll pick it up in the second half." My response was then go do it and prove that we are as good as everyone thinks we are. Fortunately, we did that and played with a lot of passion and aggressiveness. We won going away by 15 although the game got a bit chippy at the end with our point guard getting shoved into the bleachers at one point on an intentional foul. We were back at state with the #2 seed!

Our opponent was Iowa City West, defending state champions and coached by old friend BJ Mayer. Their best player was going to the University of Iowa and had been on a tear at the end of the season. We were coming off disappointing efforts in our first two state games and were determined to get the first win ever for the Mason City girls' basketball team at the state tournament.

The game was never in doubt. We came out on fire from the 3-point arc and ended up with a state tournament record 14 made 3's out of only 22 attempts! West's best player scored 31 points, but we shut down the rest of the team to win easily 72-53. What a relief to have the monkey off our back of never having won a game at state and then to win so convincingly and with a state record made it even better!

Our foe in the semifinals was a familiar face in Dowling who had hit a late three to beat Des Moines East. We knew it would be a tough game as they were tall and athletic, but we were incredibly confident coming off our first round win and having beaten them earlier in the year. Unfortunately, we got off to a rough start and got down 11 after one quarter. As we were known to do, we fought back in the second quarter and cut it to three at halftime. We had played pretty poorly and were only down three so we felt good for the rest of the game.

The third quarter was a back and forth affair until mid-quarter when we suddenly went on a tear. We hit a three to take the lead and then our point guard took over with some great plays and a couple of three's to send our crowd into a frenzy! We led by five after three and with our history of holding onto leads late in the game, we felt confident we were headed to our first ever championship game!

Unfortunately, everything unraveled in the fourth quarter. We missed our last 12 shots and Dowling totally took our point guard out of the game with a junk defense. They weren't spectacular on offense but picked away at the lead and finally took a one-point lead with just over a minute left. We turned the ball over too much and ended up having to foul. To their credit, Dowling ended the game by making nine out of ten free throws in the last minute or so of the game. One of their freshmen (a future Division I player) had 17 points, and despite an incredible effort, we went down 50-43.

It was a crushing defeat made even worse by the fact we had some players openly question our substitution patterns during the game, and one of them was very open about that with the press after the game. I heard every word, and it was incredibly disappointing to hear those words, but I was not surprised and did not respond. As a coach, I tend to second-guess myself after a loss, and it was a game I certainly wish I had a do-over with. We needed a better plan when Dowling switched up their defense. I needed better communication with the players especially in the past so that when the going got tough, there was more of a trust factor involved as well as a better ability to cope with adversity.

Looking back, I think that the Mason City team was the best in the state and should have won the title, but it wasn't meant to be. It would have been easy going forward to hold some grudges based on some of the events from that year and in the past, but after some initial bitterness, I chose to move on and try and be the better person. It took me almost a day after the loss to do this, but the next day, we ended up taking the team back down to Des Moines to watch the finals (and watch Dowling lose the championship game), and being around such great kids and getting such positive reactions from them helped ease the pain and helped me realize I was doing the right thing.

As a leader, things aren't always going to go your way and one needs to take responsibility and accountability for that as actions certainly affect the success or failure of the groups. It's OK to admit that we mess up, and I clearly messed up during the 2012-13 season as well as not coaching the group of athletes during that time like I needed to. As coaches, we are working with young people who are at different stages of maturity so we cannot expect them to make appropriate decisions and react wisely at all times. **It's up to coaches to model appropriate behavior in the good times and the bad times.** Student athletes may not agree or understand what coaches are doing at the time but hopefully at some point down the road, they will understand our actions and learn at least something from what we did to help build their own lives. My mom says at times, "You need to treat people with sugar, not vinegar." How true. **Being the better person is tougher today than ever before with social media and the easy ability to respond to criticism. What do we have to gain in life by being negative toward others and pointing out their flaws? If we all spent more time working on our own abilities and less time worrying about what others are doing, the world would be a better place.**

After this season, I did give some consideration to resigning my position and taking a break from coaching. I wondered if I would ever get a chance to win the ultimate prize, and I knew as much as anyone that the 2012-13 team was probably the best chance to win it all. Some of the issues we had dealt with in previous years had also worn me down and not having to take long bus rides in the winter was definitely inviting. However, after a number of discussions with my wife and others, I decided to keep coaching as I still had a great passion for the game and knew that I could still help kids achieve great things, and I hoped to learn from my previous mistakes. I knew we still had a lot of talent in the program, and I hoped that we could keep climbing the mountain in girls' basketball!

That spring, we found out that the school district budget was considering a number of budget cuts with regards to academics and athletics, and one of the positions under consideration was Coach Kirby's job. Considering all the success the girls' program was having, it was a difficult situation, and a lot of other quality people were under consideration for cuts. I was even part of the cuts as I had taken on a supplemental job as a professional development facilitator, and most of those positions in the district were being cut as well. That was not a big deal for me though, and we knew that would happen.

A number of community people and I as well as our senior point guard spoke at a board meeting about the importance of the coaching positions, and ultimately, the board decided to look at other options and chose to keep the coaching positions. We were elated about the outcome and hoped that this was the end of the budget issues. Interestingly, it was reported in the news that Curt Klaahsen's position was cut during the meeting -technically that was true with the professional development position, but some of my coaching friends thought I had lost my teaching and coaching jobs! In fact, a Des Moines area school coach texted me immediately saying not to worry that they had a job for me and that I could work for him! I got the word out quickly that I would not be going anywhere. Unfortunately, there were more issues to come.

CHAPTER 20

NOW WHAT?

Deciding What's Next is Always Difficult

When the 2013-14 season began, the question was "Now what?" We had made the state tournament three straight years and expectations were still high. We knew we had lost arguably the best girls' basketball class to graduate from MCHS, but we still had a number of returnees, including two starters who had committed to Division I programs, meaning we had four Division I players during those years. What a blessing to have such great kids who put so much time and effort into the sport, and how gratifying to see the success they had!

We got off to a great start that season with eight wins in our first nine games, although there were a number of struggles, and we weren't able to do the things defensively that we had done in the past. We rose to as high as #4 in the rankings although deep down, I knew that was pretty high for us and that the toughest part of our schedule was yet to come. Those fears came to fruition as our record in our last 12 games was 5-7. We struggled to beat the best teams on our schedule which made our potential tournament path even harder. On any given night, we could beat good teams, but it took our very best effort. Right before tournaments, we beat #4 Waukee at their place in a tight game, so we felt we were going in the right direction. We headed into tournaments and faced familiar foe Cedar Falls who had beaten us earlier in January. Fortunately, we were at home, but we knew it would be a tough game, and it was. We led by two going into the fourth quarter, but played a great quarter, hit some big shots and free throws and pulled it out by 10.

We were back in the regional final for the fourth straight year where we would play familiar foe Des Moines East, although we did not play them during the regular season. They were very fast and athletic as they usually were. The game was at the neutral site of Ames. We had won there earlier in the year and felt confident going in. We felt we had a good defensive plan and tried to slow down the game and play up the underdog role as East was higher-ranked, and I believe felt it would be a fairly easy game. Unfortunately, our best shooter was under the weather on game day. Despite that, we led by two and kept the game close, trailing by four going into the fourth quarter. We fought back and took a brief lead with under two minutes to play. Unfortunately, it was not meant to be. We trailed by one with 30 seconds left with the ball but turned it over and had to foul. They missed the free throw, but got the rebound and put it back in. We then turned it over again, and the clock ran out with us losing 53-50.

The locker room after the game was full of distraught players. The seniors were not only excellent players but great kids who had developed awesome relationships with my staff and me. We gave them a chance to speak and their words were powerful about how much basketball and the coaches meant to them. They talked especially about the life-long lessons they had learned and how they were so appreciative of everything that had been done for them. It was powerful stuff and was a great reminder that **win or lose, players can learn so many life lessons from sports and the least of those have to do with winning and losing. There is an old saying that coachable players become reliable employees and well-mannered adults.** I have found in my experience that statement to be so true.

We wanted to win that game so badly and because we had made state three straight years, some of the players felt they had let everyone down because of the loss. Unfortunately, **sports teach us that like life, you don't win every time, and you need to learn to deal with loss.** As in life, dealing with a loss is much easier if you are surrounded by a caring "family" that is there for you no matter what. **Surrounding ourselves with great people is a choice we all make…our friends and acquaintances are our choice…our activities are our choice.** We don't have a choice with regards to our families, but with our friends and activities, it's all on us. When you choose to be a part of and participate on a great team, you gain the benefits of those people being around you. If you choose to be a part of a negative and not a positive team, you gain the worst parts of that group.

Another thought is that you become the people that you surround yourself with. Sports gives young people a chance to be a part of a positive experience if everyone (players and coaches) buy in and create that type of team culture. The 2013-14 team definitely had that positive team culture, and I'm confident, despite the loss, it was a great life-learning experience for everyone on the team. That is the coach's goal for every team coached, and I believe that giving kids a positive, life-long learning experience is the most important thing they can gain from an athletic season. At the time, wins and losses are a life and death matter. However, in the grand scheme of things, the life lessons learned become the most important part. Hopefully our players are better able to deal with life lessons and the ups and downs because they participated on our teams.

The spring of 2014 saw a huge change with our staff. The Mohawk boys' head basketball coaching position had opened up, and my JV coach, Nick Trask, let me know he was interested in the position. Besides being my assistant, Coach Trask was an assistant football and boys' soccer coach. Add in his being a social studies teacher, he had a great relationship with many of the high school boys and had a great deal of experience for the position. Although I knew losing him on our staff would be difficult, I supported him wholeheartedly in his pursuit of the boys' position. I knew he would do a great job. His passion, knowledge, and ability to relate to student athletes ensured he would be a perfect fit for the position. If he got the job, we would deal with how to replace everything he did for the program.

I have always thought that assistant coaches should be thinking about being a head coach someday and be thinking about what they would do if they were the head coach. If they are just there for the money or are afraid of making mistakes, then they will not be very valuable to me. I have wanted/demanded honesty and loyalty from my assistants and have valued their input. I have been incredibly blessed with the work of my assistants and each has become great friends off the court.

After a long process, Coach Trask was finally named the head boys' basketball coach at Mason City. I couldn't have been prouder of someone who had grown so much as a coach and a person over the last seven years and who had been with me through all of the ups and downs of my Mason City journey. As I have gotten older, my assistants have almost become the kids I never had, which makes it even more gratifying to see the success they have. We decided to have Coach Katie Trask move up to the JV coaching position, and hired Britney Borchardt, a 2007 graduate, as our freshmen coach. We knew some roles would change, but we hoped the continuity would continue because of everything we had put together the previous seven years.

During the spring, our athletic director, Bob Kenny, notified us that because of budget concerns, a number of coaching positions were under consideration for being cut, and once again, Coach Kirby's position was one that was on the line. The head coaches and I along with booster representatives met to try and figure out how to make up the $30,000 cuts that the district wanted. We came up with a plan that I helped present to Superintendent Anita Micich that we hoped would keep the positions. I received a call from Dr. Micich on a Saturday night (I was with the Fire in Minneapolis) saying she was pleased to let me know the board would accept our proposal and that no positions would be cut. She also asked if I would make a statement at the board meeting that Monday night about how we worked together to resolve the cuts, and I agreed to do that. In fact, I typed up a statement and sent it to Dr. Micich before the meeting so that she knew exactly what I would say as I am a huge proponent of being upfront with people and did not want anyone to be surprised by what was said.

On Monday morning, I was surprised to see a district email from Bob Kenny saying that it was going to be proposed at the board meeting that his position as activities director be cut. Wait, what? I thought the budget issues were done! I immediately emailed Dr. Micich that I would not be reading my statement to the board but would instead would be supporting Bob to keep his AD position.

She thanked me and said she would send my original statement to the board members which is something I thought was odd. I then typed my remarks and sent them to Dr. Micich again ahead of time to continue to be upfront with my words.

Bob sent his email to people throughout the state and community. As you would expect, a large group of citizens and athletes showed up in support of keeping his position. I was one of a number of speakers, and each one was in agreement of keeping the position. It was an easy speech to make as Bob had done an excellent job, was a great supporter of mine, and overall, eliminating the position with no plan of how to replace the duties was crazy in my mind. The board quickly decided to keep Bob's position, but in many ways, it made us a laughingstock throughout the state as I probably had 20 or more people contact me and ask, "What the heck is Mason City doing up there?"

It was a no-brainer in going public and speaking up for not only the AD position but Coach Kirby and the other positions as well. I am going to support people doing a great job as well as supporting the importance of keeping those who work with young people to continue to give students the extra opportunities they deserve. I will stand up for what I feel is right and if that upsets people, that is OK, as everyone is entitled to his/her opinions. It upsets me that civil disagreements seem to the be norm today. More often than not, differences of opinion turn into name-calling, personal vindictives, and other questionable behaviors. We need to be able to disagree without being disagreeable.

Overall, it's probably fair to say that a part of my leadership style is being non-confrontational. It doesn't mean I won't stand up for what I believe in. I refuse to get drawn into public disagreements and would much rather try to solve things behind the scenes and in a quieter fashion. It's like people feel that the louder and more out in the open they are, the better chance they have of being correct with regards to public opinion. I disagree!

The spring and summer of 2014 were a busy time for me personally as we found out the *Des Moines Register's* great bike ride across Iowa (RAGBRAI) was going to be staying overnight in Mason City on Wednesday, July 23rd. Our school district's superintendent was on the RAGBRAI committee in town and called to ask if I would consider being the chairman of the volunteer committee which was a huge undertaking! I knew a lot about it as my Uncle Jr, and his son, Jack Stubbe, were long-time employees of the Register and had been a part of the bike ride almost from the beginning. Despite knowing a lot of work was ahead, and we were told we might need up to 1000 volunteers, I decided to accept the position. We also had some friends from Cherokee ask if they could stay overnight with us so there was a lot going on.

There was also a lot to learn and a lot of meetings, but I thoroughly enjoyed my time helping with RAGBRAI. I met a number of city leaders and community leaders dedicated to making it a great event. I spent much of my spring and summer attending events to recruit volunteers as well as planning with the other committees as my job was to help supply them with volunteers. Our North Iowa Fire group was asked to help with the recycling cans part of the operation so I also spent time trying to make sure that was ready to go as well.

July 23rd came and although I really didn't get a chance to enjoy the day because of running around checking on everything, the day was a spectacular success in all areas. Fortunately, all of the volunteers showed up and did a great job. We received much feedback that we had by far the best stop on the trip as well as the best volunteers. The volunteer shirts were a huge hit, and I had a number of people offer to pay $20 or more for the shirt off my back! Rocker Bret Michaels was the main entertainment and word was that close to 20,000 people packed the downtown area!

Although it was a ton of work and took up much of my summer, I have no regrets about taking on the volunteer position for RAGBRAI. **I believe it is vital that we all step up when help is needed and do what we can to support our communities.** I often feel I don't do enough to volunteer with everything else we have going on, but hopefully I can do more of that when I retire.

As we entered the 2014-15 basketball season, expectations were down a bit. We had lost another great class, we only had three seniors, and we had to replace Coach Nick Trask. That fall, one of our seniors (a key contributor the year before), had surgery on her hip and was out for the season. Fortunately, she became a great manager, but it meant we had a lot to replace. We had two starters returning, but a lot of inexperience after that. Probably because of previous success, the union ranked us 10th to start the year. That was somewhat laughable to me based on all of our losses, but we hoped to play our best at the end of the year which has been a trend of ours.

We got off to a 3-1 start before getting drilled by Valley. That led to a stretch of four losses in five games, putting us at 4-5 for the season. We again struggled against the best CIML teams as their speed and strength were too much for us. One of those losses was against Ankeny Centennial at home where we were tied going into the fourth quarter, then proceeded to miss all 14 of our shots in the quarter, went scoreless, and then lost 51-35. Fortunately, we would see Centennial again.

After a lopsided loss to Cedar Falls in mid-January, we were 7-7 and struggling. However, we knew the schedule was going to get a bit easier, and we had a chance to get on a good roll. Fortunately, we did, winning six of our last seven regular season games, with the only loss, a tough one to Waukee, where we fought to the end. We were 13-8 at this time and felt pretty good about things although we knew we were an underdog.

The girls' union had changed up tournament play a bit. Basically, the higher-seeded teams hosted all tournament games. We were fortunately the second seed, which meant we would be playing our nemesis Des Moines East at home. We had beaten them earlier in the year, but they had been really young, and their best player had missed the first game, so we knew it was going to be a battle. They were also very athletic like usual, and that always gave us trouble. A battle it was! East was not a great shooting team going into tournaments, but of course they shot well this game and hit five 3-pointers. We led most of the game and by six at halftime and after three quarters. However, they kept fighting and cut it to one with under 10 seconds left. We hit two free throws to lead by three when they came down and after some chaos, threw up a wild shot from the corner which was nothing but net.

Our players were pretty discouraged coming to the bench, but my advice to them was pretty simple, "We haven't done anything easily all year so why would we change now?" If there is one thing I think our team has done pretty well most of the time over the years, it has been staying calm under pressure and handling late game situations. Fortunately, we came out and hit a three 10 seconds going into overtime and led the rest of the way. However, East kept battling, and cut it to two with 10 seconds left. After a turnover and a free throw from us, this time they missed the final three and we won 63-60 to head back to the regional final for the fifth straight year.

One of the keys as a coach during hectic games is to stay as calm as possible. Most of the time, teams take on the disposition of their coach, and I believe that in close games, if I am all nervous and yelling at the players, they will react accordingly. **People in general respond better to calm, positive leadership than emotional or angry leadership.** That doesn't mean I don't get excited at times, but at crucial moments, someone needs to be leading, and someone needs to be thinking and focused on what needs to be done. Doing this requires continued feedback to players but keeping them positive as well. When I think about times when my teams have failed in pressure situations, I feel I did not do a good enough job of putting them in the right positions and staying positive. I think I got too caught up in the moment when my players needed me to guide and support them through those times. As I like to say, "Someone has to be the adult in those situations," and it needs to be the leader in charge! Honestly, I try to give my teams what they need. If I feel they need me to stay calm, I do that. If I feel they need some extra motivation, I get a little more excited. **Overall, coaches need consistency, but we need to be receptive to the needs of our players as well.**

The #1 seed in our regional was Centennial, and unfortunately, the game

138

would be in their gym. We had played them even for three quarters, so we knew we could play with them, but we also knew it would be tough. They would have the home court advantage, but I knew it wouldn't be a normal home game for them. Usually on the road in the CIML, you have parents supporting you with very few students. I knew our student section would support us, and the sound in the gym would definitely be different, and Centennial would have to adjust. I was right! Our students showed up, sat right behind us, and made a ton of noise before the game. Centennial was a young team, and it had to have some effect. Plus, they were the #4 ranked team and expected to win. Those are very tough expectations for young teams to fight through.

It was a back and forth the first quarter and we were down by four. However, the second quarter was all Mohawks as we knocked down six out of nine three-pointers in the first half to lead by six at halftime. We pushed the lead to 12 after the half, but Centennial battled back in the third. We still led by five as they made a 7-0 run at the end of the third. Fortunately, one of our juniors (and quietest players) hit two straight 3's to start the fourth quarter and suddenly we were up 12, and we were close to a huge upset!

A side note to that game is that at the end of the third quarter, their student section that had been very quiet and almost not as big as ours tried to move directly under our basket so they could distract our shooters. The Centennial AD (ironically, the former Fort Dodge AD who we had an issue with during a regional final a few years ago) stepped forward and told his students to return to their seats, making sure it stayed fair throughout the game. What a classy and gutsy move on his part. We found out after the game that a number of Centennial parents had ripped on him for hurting the team and possibly keeping them from winning! I made sure I found him after the game when our team was the only people left to let him know how much I appreciated that and admired his integrity with taking the action he did.

The last five minutes of the game seemed to take five hours. Centennial went to a full-court press which we struggled with at times. There were also a lot of deflections out of bounds, and we had to use all of our timeouts with over a minute left. I try to save timeouts for the end of the game unless they are desperately needed earlier so fortunately, we had them to use at the end. I had been calm the entire game, but toward the end, when we hit a couple of free throws to wrap it up, I became probably as excited and as emotional as I had ever been at the end of a game. For this team to advance to state considering the circumstances and how much we had struggled during the season, it might have been one of my proudest coaching moments. This team probably wasn't as talented as some of our previous teams, but they stuck together, believed in themselves, their teammates, and their coaches, and came through in the clutch when they needed to for the good of the team. I also think the staff and I did one of our best jobs of keeping a fairly young team together and positive despite all of the adversity.

After the mad celebration at the end of the game and finding my wife and family, the first person I tracked down was Coach Nick Trask and gave him a big bear hug. He had tears in his eyes and expressed how proud he was. I let him know how important he was to our program and that he was a big part of the reason we were going back to state. I asked him to come with us and be a part of our "scout team" for the state game. He had a huge part in breaking down tape and showing the players what our opponent could do. I knew it was tough for him to not be on the staff any more, but I definitely wanted him to know how important he was.

Once we saw the scores, we knew our opponent at state would be #1 Valley, who had beaten us pretty handily earlier in the year. They were very talented and well-coached, but we thought we had a good shot at them with the way we were playing. Unfortunately, it did not turn out that way. Valley jumped on us early, we turned it over a lot (23 for the game), and shot just 5 for 25 from the 3-point line despite having good shots. They were clearly the better team and showed it by winning 65-42. We never led, and it clearly wasn't meant to be.

However, nothing could take away from what that team accomplished with a fourth state tournament in five years, upsetting Centennial on the road, having only two seniors, and much more. The fact we had 13 returning players gave everyone hope for the future, and we knew we had another good freshman class coming into the program. Also, in the spring, the classifications came out from the union letting us know that we would be dropping down a class to 4A instead of 5A. Basically, we would keep the same conference schedule we had in previous years, but in tournaments, we would play slightly smaller schools. No more Centennial, DM East, or Valley, who had more than three times the students we had. Certainly everyone was excited about that, and if I had a dollar for every time someone that summer said, "Coach, you are going to win state this year," I might have been able to retire early! Unfortunately, our players heard the same thing. At our summer camp, when I asked players how many had been told we were going to win state, every hand went up.

Fortunately, we went to a couple of team camps where we played many smaller schools and some in class 4A. Some of those teams beat us soundly. Granted, not all of our players were there, but it still emphasized the point that there were really good teams in all classes and without work, we had no chance of winning state. That was clearly the goal, but we knew it would not be easy. Little did I know how difficult that next season and that next year would be.

CHAPTER 21

IT WAS THE BEST OF TIMES, IT WAS THE WORST OF TIMES CHARLES DICKENS

Challenges Lead to Strength

2015 was one of the most difficult years I have personally experienced. The year started with the loss of my Uncle Roger followed closely by the passing of my Aunt Chyrl (they were not married to each other). Both had battled health issues, but it was difficult to lose them and all of the positive memories I had of them growing up and all of the family gatherings we had. The only positive was being able to see our cousins that I hadn't seen in a long time. I just wish it had been under better circumstances.

Chyrl's son Don battled pancreatic cancer and passed away that summer. Don had served in the Navy for 20 years so he was tough and had been through a lot. He had cut my hair for all of my years at Cherokee, and we used to drive to Don's house for a haircut about 30 minutes away and a great visit. The folks would often drive over from George, and it was always a great time. Don had an awesome sense of humor and was almost like another brother to our family. Then, only a day after Don's funeral, we received word that his sister Marlene had passed away suddenly in Arizona. Marlene had come back for her mom's funeral but wasn't up to making it back for Don's. We also lost a couple of family friends during that time as well, so it was a very tough stretch.

On top of that, in early May I received a call from my sister that Dad had been stricken with a heart attack and had been taken to the hospital. We had been back to George the week before for his birthday, and Margo and I had commented that he seemed pretty labored when he walked, more so than usual. He was his usual jovial self, but definitely seemed to lack energy. His condition was stable, but he was transferred to the Sioux Falls Avera Heart Hospital where they would be performing an angiogram on Saturday morning to check things out. I decided to go to Sioux Falls early that morning, and Margo stayed home as she was not feeling the best. By the time I got there, the test was over and the heart doctor came out to talk to Mom and all of us kids. His news was not good as Dad had a large blockage in a major artery to the heart and with his age, there were two options of either bypass surgery, or he would go to Hospice. With surgery and his age, the chances of him surviving weren't great, and the surgery itself would be difficult. Without surgery, he would not survive long. Wow...that was a blow, and we all were taken aback.

Obviously, we kids thought that surgery was the best option, and it should get done. Mom said emphatically that as long as he was cognizant of what was going on, he would make the final decision. Dad had always said that he did not want to be kept alive on a ventilator, and we all agreed we did not want him to suffer. He was resting comfortably so it was decided I would run Mom back to George about an hour away so she could get some clothes and pills since Dad would be in Sioux Falls for a while. We made it there and were on our way back when brother Steve called, asking repeatedly when we would be back, that "Dad needed Mom." He didn't say much more, but you could tell he was nervous.

We got back and were met at the front door by my siblings explaining that Dad had experienced a lot of breathing problems, and they were concerned whether he would make it through the day. When we walked in, things had calmed down, but it was definitely serious. Mom visited a while with Dad, and he decided that he wasn't sure about the surgery and might not want to go through it. It was decided to wait until morning and discuss everything some more. Mom and I decided to get a room at the motel attached to the hospital (great concept) and everyone else went home until early the next morning.

Sunday morning, Mom and I headed to Dad's room early, and when we walked in, they were just calling us to come as he was having another bad episode. His doctor happened to be right there and helped get everything stabilized. Mom had another conversation with Dad, and he decided he would go through with the surgery. We were concerned about waiting until Monday for surgery with the increasing episodes and the obvious trauma it was causing Dad.

The heart surgeon happened to be in the building, and he was called in to evaluate Dad. Fortunately, the rest of the family made it by then, and we all heard the surgeon. After a short time, he was very blunt about telling us that surgery was very risky and the odds of him surviving were not good. Without surgery, Dad would not survive long. The doctor and the surgeon conversed for a time, and when they got done, asked Dad what he wanted to do. Dad said he would have the surgery. I asked them when surgery would be, and they said, "Right now." Another wow. We literally had a few minutes to say good luck and that we loved him, and they were wheeling him out. It was such a whirlwind, but we all were content with the decision for surgery. Dad made it with a clear mind, and he was also clear that he might not make it. His faith was strong as was his faith in the doctors.

We went to the waiting room and tried to contact other family members as well as make time pass as quickly as possible. It was a really tough day waiting, but we all put our faith in God and waited for the results. When the surgeon came out, he said everything went well, and he was guardedly optimistic, but there was a long way to go. It was at that point that Mom broke down and cried for the first time. I think it was more about the relief of it than anything else. I decided then to stay for the week as we knew Dad would be there for at least that long. We thought that it was best for Margo to stay home and her folks met me halfway on Monday and delivered some clothes.

Dad made steady progress and eventually was dismissed to the Rock Rapids Hospital for rehab. Almost miraculously, he was able to go home, and although slowed down, he had a good summer and was looking pretty good. We were so blessed with this extended time with him, and he continued to have an amazing spirit and sense of humor about everything. It would have been easy to give up or complain about everything, but he never did. Things went well until mid-August, when I got a call on a Saturday night that Dad was unresponsive, and they were taking him to the hospital. Margo and I waited for news, and we started getting ready to possibly head to Rock Rapids. We talked to brother Steve who said things weren't too good and Dad wasn't responding. The doctor was telling them he wasn't sure if he would come out of it.

We made the decision to head to Rock Rapids, despite it being after midnight. We arrived in Rock Rapids to Dad still being unresponsive, and we assumed that this might be it. We debated whether he should be taken to Sioux Falls, and my siblings and I questioned why that hadn't been done yet. Mom and the doctor questioned if it was worth it. The discussion continued when suddenly Dad came out of his "coma" and was able to communicate with us, and it was clear he knew what was going on. Mom talked to him again, and he agreed to head to Sioux Falls. We followed him to the ambulance, and he gave us all a big thumbs up from the back of the ambulance...amazing! It was after 6:30 by the time we arrived in Sioux Falls. Everyone was exhausted, and Margo was starting to get a bad migraine. We finally got her to Larry and Mary Jane's place in Sioux Falls so she could sleep, but she was in a lot of pain.

Meanwhile, back at the hospital, tests showed that Dad was stable, and he was joking around at times and able to communicate with us. It was made clear to us that he had congestive heart failure and that there was little more that could be done for him. He could survive for a while or for a short time, and there really wasn't any knowing about which it would be. It was decided that he would head back to the Rock Rapids swing bed when he was able.

On Sunday afternoon, I headed back to Margo, and she was really struggling. The headache was unbearable, and she had been throwing up at times. She tried to sleep, but the symptoms continued. Finally, close to midnight, we made the decision to take her to the ER. After some research and talking to Larry and Mary Jane, we discovered the heart hospital's ER was for all patients and was very good. After we arrived, they hooked her up to IV's and gave her medicine. After a few hours, she started to feel much better, and it was decided she would be dismissed. Interestingly, Dad's room was just above the ER, so before we

143

left, I decided to head up and check on him and Mom who was determined to sleep in his room. They were both snoring away so I headed back out, and we first stopped at McDonald's because Margo was hungry and then headed to Larry's. What a stretch it had been! Dad eventually made it to Rock Rapids and then was transferred to the nursing home in George. He was stable at the time, and the hope was to be able to get him to be able to return home at some point. Unfortunately, that never happened.

One of the most interesting people we met in Sioux Falls at Avera Heart was a man named Jon Soderholm. The day after Dad's surgery, Mom and I were sitting in the waiting room while the nurses were working with Dad when a voice came over the intercom. "Good morning; this is Jon." Jon proceeded to then have a short, positive message about life, and then ended by reciting the Pledge of Allegiance. His words were very uplifting, and I was impressed that he used the Pledge. We had just started having our students at the middle school recite it so it was great to hear it in another area!

Shortly after the message, a gentleman came walking down the hallway greeting people with a plate full of freshly baked cookies. He stopped by Mom and me and not only offered cookies but also recognized we had not been here previously and asked questions about why we were there. We discussed Dad's condition, and he asked questions while showing a genuine concern. When we asked his name, he simply said Jon. When I asked if he was the Jon from the earlier message, he said yes, and that he enjoyed doing that every day. I mentioned that our middle school did the Pledge, and he was impressed with that forward thinking! Jon then said he had more cookies to deliver, and he would keep checking in about Dad's condition.

Every day that week, at the beginning of the day at Avera Heart, there would be a message from Jon followed shortly by the delivery of cookies. After the first day, he knew us by name and stopped by to see Dad as well. On the Saturday before Dad was dismissed, we saw Jon again. He mentioned that he wasn't supposed to be working but thought he would stop by and see how things were going with everyone at the hospital. We finally decided to ask what Jon's official job was at Avera Heart. He was the CEO of the whole hospital! Talk about fantastic leadership, caring about people, and providing a quality product. How many CEO's would go the extra mile like Jon did? **What would happen in the world of hospitals, businesses, schools, etc. if the leader was as visible as Jon and as people-driven as Jon was?**

Obviously, over the span of my life and my career, I have seen a number of leaders like Jon, and it always shows up in the quality of the work done by their business or school. **The question is why can't we get more leaders to see the big picture and go above and beyond like Jon does? Think about the impact on customers, students, and employees if more CEO's followed**

the path that Jon does in his daily work.

The end of August meant the start of school so once we got back from Dad's hospitalization, school was starting up. September 1st, my first day back, was a blur. It was an all-district meeting so it was great to see so many friends I hadn't seen for the summer. However, I don't have a clue what was talked about at the meeting as my mind was still three hours away.

The first familiar face I saw was Hutch, Jennifer Hutchens, who immediately gave me a hug and asked how Dad was doing and specifically how I was doing. She reminded me to take care of myself and to let her know if there was anything she could do to help. Hutch was the consummate professional as a special education educator and was a better human being. I co-taught with her for three years, and there was never a dull moment. She had a special way with kids and how best to teach them. Everything was out in the open with her, and there was very little filter on what she said! Until our schedules changed, I spent a few years eating lunch with our seventh grade team and without giving details, nothing was off the table with regards to discussions. The talks would range from romances, female problems "down there," politics, and anything else. If Hutch didn't get an answer she desired, she would lead the charge for the truth!

One day in social studies class, we were working on geography and the four cardinal directions of north, south, east, and west. Hutch loved to have kids use acronyms and metaphors to help them remember key points. When a student asked her once how to remember which direction was which, she said NESW-Never Ever Smoke Weed! HA! That was a typical Hutch response.

Hutch made everyone she met feel like a great friend even after a short period of time and was always concerned about how you were doing. Her students were everything to her, and Hutch went above and beyond to make sure students received the help that they needed. The same was true with her family and friends, and it's what made her beloved by everyone she met.

I didn't see her much when school started as we were not co-teaching any more. I noted that she missed school on Friday and was told that she wasn't feeling the best. Her birthday was Saturday the 5th so I hoped she would be feeling better. On Saturday morning, I texted her happy birthday greetings to " 'you 'ole bag' " which was one of her favorite sayings and hoped she was feeling better! I didn't get a response and didn't think anything else of it. Saturday night I was home when I received a call from my great friend and colleague Anne Brown telling me "Hutch has passed away." Words cannot describe the shock and sadness that I felt. How did this happen? How could she be gone? I will not go into the causes of her passing, but it just added to the disbelief.

On Sunday, a number of her friends and colleagues gathered at Clear Lake to be together and mourn Hutch's passing. Not a lot of words were said. I don't think anyone knew what to say. Our JAMS staff met on Monday evening (Labor Day) to discuss plans and the level of sadness was almost overwhelming. There was a celebration of life for Hutch on Saturday. It was a beautiful service and all of the eloquent speakers showed how much she meant to so many. Words many times cannot paint a true picture of the life a person has led, but the speakers hit on that perfectly. It was great to connect with people who knew her outside the school system and to hear about the many things they shared. My wife and I had a long conversation with Hutch's husband John after the service, and it was obvious how grateful he was to everyone and how it helped him realize the impact she had on so many. I have no idea how he could remain so strong after losing the love of his life. I was still in a fog and could only imagine.

So what lessons can all of us learn from this wonderful life that ended way too soon? Here are a few that are necessary to mention:

1. **Relationships, relationships, relationships.** Hutch had great connections to kids, school personnel, former classmates, and relatives. You name it. That wasn't by accident. She worked hard at that EVERY DAY! She made sure to connect with her group of UNI friends every year since they graduated!

2. **Live your life with passion.** Hutch brought passion to everything she did. She gave it her all every day with every situation and person she dealt with. She co-taught with me for three years and was basically thrown into the situation. The first day she told me, "I don't know a damn thing about social studies, but we will work hard at it and we will have fun." That we did! I learned a great deal from her about working with kids, and especially kids who had special needs or needed extra help.

3. **Treat everyone the same.** It didn't matter what your title was or what kind of student you were, Hutch treated everyone like they were the most important person in the world. It didn't matter if you were an administrator/teacher/para, or an A student or D student. She cared about everyone the same, and had fun with all the same. If you were not the subject of one of her pranks or jokes, you were in the minority!

4. **Don't live your life by a time clock.** Many days, Hutch was at school well before her contracted time of 8:00 and stayed much later than she had to at 4:00. If something needed to be done, she made sure she stayed to get it done. Going above and beyond is OK at times.

5. **Have fun.** There was never a dull moment with Hutch. She found a way to make lunch entertaining, PD meetings entertaining, and classes entertaining. It didn't matter. Her unique sense of humor was contagious.

I'm not sure any of us who knew and loved Hutch will ever get over her passing, but she would want us to "keep on keepin' on" and live our lives to the fullest. It will never be the same without her around though.

Going back to school was very difficult without Hutch, but fortunately I was surrounded by amazing co-workers including people who had recently retired but still stayed close to all of us. Somehow we made it through those difficult weeks together, and I'm so thankful that each one of them has been a part of my life. They are not only great teachers, but also amazing people who are in it for the right reasons. One of my favorite phrases is that **we should do what we can to surround ourselves with great people who will be there when we need them and keep our life under balance.** You can tell a lot about people based on their friends, and in that sense, I am looking great!

Meanwhile, Dad's health was continuing to deteriorate. We knew that he was not going to get better, but it was still difficult to see this incredibly tough, caring man go down hill and be unable to function like he had been doing. He continued to have episodes where he was unresponsive, and every time I went back to see him, it was clear things were getting worse.

Throughout these days, Mom was constantly by Dad's side, helping him with meals, wheeling him out so he could visit with other residents, and making sure the nursing home was doing everything they were supposed to be doing for him. Fortunately, the nursing home was in George so Mom could go home every night to get some sleep and could run in whenever needed. Words cannot describe the quality of care and attention to detail that Mom gave to Dad for so many years. There is no doubt in my mind that without her care, we would have lost him a lot sooner than we did. She was acutely aware of how he was doing and especially during his time in the hospital and the nursing home, she made sure that every protocol was followed.

Overall, the quality of care Dad received from doctors, nurses, and other caregivers was tremendous. So many amazing people helped him continue to live and besides their knowledge, it was their bedside manner that was so impressive. Yes, we saw the other side as well at times, but the majority of the time, the care he received was top quality.

Mom's big hope was to have Dad go home at some point and maybe spend the rest of his days there. Originally, that was used as an incentive, but it was clear toward the end that it didn't make any difference. There was no way Mom could have handled everything at home with him by herself and at least we knew there were people taking care of him 24/7.

On the evening of Wednesday, October 7th, I got a call from Mom that things were not the best with Dad and that he was not very responsive again.

When I asked if she thought I should head back, she didn't really respond so usually that was a sign that the answer was yes. I decided to take the next day off from school and said I would get there in the morning. Something told me I needed to head back and see Dad, and I'm certainly glad I did. Since I don't tend to sleep for long stretches, I was up early on the 8th and decided to head to George. As always, I emailed Mom so she knew when I would arrive. She emailed back that she had not heard from the nursing home yet so she was happy about that.

I had a nice drive on a beautiful day, and I kept going until finally taking a pit stop in Sheldon about 20 minutes from George. As I walked into the convenience store, I suddenly heard my name being called. I turned to look, and it was Tim Gallagher, a reporter for the newspaper in Sioux City, someone I saw frequently when I was at Newell-Fonda, and he was in Storm Lake. We had a great conversation, and I filled him in on my reasons for being in the area. We probably talked 15 minutes, and then I headed back to my vehicle.

When I got in, I looked at my phone and saw that Mom had called 10 minutes ago. Uh oh. I called back, and she asked where I was. I replied and she said, "Things aren't good; Dad will not make it through the day." I made my way to George and saw that she was right. Dad was not conscious but did not appear to be in pain either which we were thankful for at this difficult time. Fortunately, my brother Steve and sister Marianne lived in town and came right away. Brother Larry and Mary Jane lived in Sioux Falls, and Mom said they were on their way, and they arrived about 10:00. We took turns sitting by Dad and reassuring him everything was OK, we would all be fine, and he didn't need to worry.

About 11:00, the nursing home staff came in and said they needed to turn Dad as he was on his side. We all stepped out and soon after the staff came back and said, "You need to go back in; he is going fast." We went back into the room, told him we loved him, and soon after that he was gone. It was the toughest moment of my life, but it was made a little easier by being surrounded by people I loved, and knowing that Dad was in a better place, and that he did not suffer. Mom was incredibly strong, and she was making sure we were all OK when it should have been the other way around.

One of the most touching things that happened was when the nursing home staff who had taken care of Dad all came in and held a brief memorial service for him with scripture, encouraging words, and a chance for family and staff to share their recollections. What a great blessing to do for family, and it helped ease the immediate pain a bit. It makes you think how hard it must be for caregivers like that when someone passes away. If they are doing their job well, they undoubtedly become attached to their patients and many times see those patients pass away. It's amazing how they deal emotionally with those losses, and

I personally can't thank caregivers enough for everything they do.

We met immediately with the funeral home to work on arrangements and a date for the funeral. To add onto the sadness, the folks' former pastor and neighbor for nine years, Dave Vander Laan, had passed away on the 7th after a long battle with cancer. He was an amazing man and so good to both Dad and Mom. You could always rely on a birthday message from him with "God Delights in You" on it. Pastor Dave's funeral was scheduled for Monday, and there was no way we would go that day. Also, Saturday was too fast, so we decided on Tuesday the 13th for the funeral and the night before for the visitation.

The folks' church did not have a minister, but fortunately, Al Honken, a former pastor, lived in the area and generously agreed to officiate the service. Pastor Al came to the folks' house on Friday and helped with arrangements for the service. The folks had talked previously about the basics of the service so planning was pretty easy. One of the items we talked about was whether to have someone do a eulogy, which we all felt was needed. During many of my trips back to George in the previous few months, I had thought about what Dad meant to people and had actually jotted down ideas in case someone did a eulogy. I decided that although I knew it would be difficult to speak at the funeral, Dad deserved it, and I felt I could make it through the speech. I took some ideas from my family, put some ideas together with mine and was happy with what I was going to present.

Obviously, funeral arrangements are highly personal and extremely emotional at times. I thought the family handled everything well. The only issue we had was putting picture displays together and how many pictures should each family have? It was more of an issue with grandkids and great grandkids. Margo and I felt it shouldn't have been a big deal as everything should have been to honor Dad and nothing else mattered. Everything else was minor to us.

One of the amazing parts of that week for me was all of the people from my present and past who reached out in so many ways whether it was calls, texts, cards, social media, or visits. There were so many people at the visitation that we stayed an hour longer than expected. Many of my friends and colleagues from Mason City, Newell, and Cherokee drove three hours or more one way just to pay respects. There were an overwhelming number of floral displays as well with many from Mason City. The next day at the funeral, there was another large group (including all of my assistants) who gave up personal days and sacrificed so much to drive that distance to be there for the family and me. Words cannot express my gratitude to everyone and the support they gave us during that time. There is no way we can ever repay what people did for us.

The day of the funeral, I felt confident in the eulogy and knew I had to deliver to give Dad the honor he deserved. I definitely felt nervous ahead of time, but I think my family was more nervous about it than I was. However, right before I was to speak, I felt something come over me. It was as if Dad was there like he always was, giving his stamp of approval and telling me that everything would be OK. I made it through the speech without breaking down and believe that it showed Dad the respect he deserved. Since Dad was a Korean War Vet, he received full military honors at the cemetery. While it was incredibly sad, it was also incredibly powerful and a perfect last salute and show of respect for the life Dad led. We can never say thank you enough to all of the Vets who have served and continue to serve our country.

It was humbling throughout the days after Dad passed to hear the stories about what he meant to people and how sad they were he was gone. Here was a quiet, humble, unassuming farmer who impacted so many people in such a positive way. I'm sure he was blushing a little up in Heaven listening to the stories as he never wanted the spotlight on himself and always made it about others. It was a fitting period of mourning and tribute for him!

I thought I would share some of the characteristics of Dad's that made him a great man and lessons that we can all do more of going forward. Some of this I shared in his eulogy. First of all, he was HUMBLE. It was never about him, but always about his family, his friends, and anyone else he met. As a friend of mine once said, "Your dad doesn't say much but when he does, you know it is something important." People tend to respect others who don't make it all about themselves.

Secondly, Dad was TOUGH. He spent two years in a combat zone in Korea and was away from his wife much of that time. He watched a buddy get killed on his own 22nd birthday. He slept in bunkers in sleeping bags on rocks and with rats running around. Later in life, Dad battled cancer (which forced him to carry a bag for urine the last 12 1/2 years of his life), heart issues, "arthur" (arthritis), and other ailments. I'm sure he complained to Mom at times, but he never let his friends and family know how difficult it was. Complaining was not on his list.

Third on the list is that despite the tough times, Dad was always POSITIVE and kept up his SENSE of HUMOR. I had a nurse comment to me one time that he was one of the only patients she had who made HER feel better after going into his room. Usually she had to make patients feel better. He had a smile for visitors and joked with everyone he knew. He loved to call the grandkids and great grandkids fake names like Jake or Dude just to make them laugh.

Next, anyone who knew Dad knew how LOYAL he was. His car had over 200,000 miles on it, he lived in the same house for 53 years, he loved wearing his favorite overalls, and he wore hats that represented the event he was attending. The only vehicles he cared about were John Deere tractors (we could open a business with his collection!), and the only cars he cared about were Chevys. Dad's biggest show of loyalty was his devotion to his loving wife of almost 64 years. Their marriage had many trials and tribulations (many involved my siblings), but he remained loyal to the end.

Lastly, and probably the biggest characteristic of Dad's that made him so beloved was the LOVE he had for his family. Nothing was more important to him. He loved family gatherings and spending time with immediate and extended family. As my brother Steve said, "Dad's wealth came in the enjoyment of his family." He was an amazing supporter of any family member's activities (although he may have been a bit hard on some referees by letting them know in German that they had messed up!) and personally attended as many as possible until his health didn't allow it.

My parents were legendary for listening to games on the radio or Internet, and if that didn't work, they would head to the car and brings snacks and drinks just to make sure they could hear the game. If they couldn't make an event, they expected a call with results and you could always count on a "Congratulations on the win" from Dad or a "You'll get the next one" if we weren't successful. As stated earlier, Mom shared a story in the days before the funeral about a time when the folks were in the car trying to listen to a game. It wouldn't come in so they kept driving. It still wouldn't come in and they kept going. Eventually, they realized they were just outside Cherokee, which was an hour away and was where we were playing! Instead of staying, they drove around our house, went home, and never told me about it!

Humility, Toughness, Humor, Positivity, Loyalty, and Love of family. How blessed we were to learn these qualities from this awesome man. We are very sad and will always miss him, but he would want us to keep living and use the qualities he exhibited. Despite never being a "coach," he was the best coach I ever had! Well done, Dad. We love and miss you, and we will do our best to uphold the qualities you taught us so well!

Not surprisingly, the most resilient, thoughtful, positive, and patient person during all of this was Mom. I think there was some relief that Dad was no longer in pain and suffering, but she was who she always was in the person thinking about others and much more worried about them than herself. You can always tell the most about someone when they are going through their biggest trial and tribulation, and Mom didn't change even at this most difficult point of her life. I took a week off from school and spent a lot of extra time with Mom, and it will be some of the most cherished times of my life. I am continuously amazed at her resiliency and ability to move on and be led by her faith. She made everyone else feel better about losing Dad when we should have been the ones making her feel better. She has been a role model for all of us to follow about how to live a proper life and how to deal with adversity that comes up. I ended up staying in George for a few more days while Margo went back to Mason City with her parents. It was a lot of quality time with Mom, and I continued to be amazed by her strength and resilience despite everything that had happened. As always, she was more worried about everyone else and said she was doing fine. Her strong faith was a big part of that and what an amazing role model she was and continues to be for all of us.

I finally went back to school on Friday the 16th. When I walked in my classroom, almost immediately, I was met by Coach Kirby and a large number of my players, bearing gifts and hugs! A number of them had sent texts earlier as well, and had expressed how Dad now had a great seat as we went after a state championship! It just showed again what a great group of people I was blessed to work with in this profession. Soon after, a number of staff members dropped by, many with diet cokes, my favorite snack treats, candy bars, and other items. I truly worked with an amazing group and despite how hard the year had already been, we were always there for each other, and I will be forever grateful for everything people did for my family and me during that awful week in October. I'm not sure what I would have done without all of the support. Little did I know that things would get drastically better from here!

CHAPTER 22

WINNING IT ALL

Finally Ending a Season Without a Loss

Getting back into a routine was difficult but returning to a more normal schedule and activities helped me get through the pain and sadness I felt. With the basketball season around the corner, it was time to shift focus and get ready for another great season.

When basketball season started in 2015, expectations were certainly high. The state named us the pre-season #1 team in class 4A and talk was still about how we were going to romp through the season. I was probably the only person not overly excited about all of the talk as I knew the regular season would humble us at some point. We did get off to an excellent start by winning five of our first six games, including a great comeback win against Valley. We were down 16 and ended the game on a 20-3 run. On the last possession, we were down one when our all-state player dribbled around and threw up a 35-foot shot that hit the rim and bounced to her freshman sister, who put the ball back in at the buzzer!

However, it was a tough stretch after that as we lost six of our next eight, including some lopsided losses against Centennial, Dowling, and Cedar Falls. After the CF loss, we were 7-7. This was interesting as that was the same record and situation the previous year when we went on a run. We decided to clear the slate and pleaded with the team to go 1-0 seven times. We again said to keep the big picture, keep the state tournament run in mind and just work to be as ready as possible when tournaments start.

About this time, we found out our tournament pairings and with the changes from the girls' union, we knew we had to finish strong if we wanted to have both of our tournament games at home. This would be a huge advantage if we could do it. We proceeded to win our next six games by shoring up our defense, finalizing our rotation, and getting people to buy in to their role. We went into our last regular season game at Waukee (a makeup game on a Monday night) ranked one spot ahead of Waverly-Shell Rock with one more ranking to come. We were concerned that if we lost, they might drop us below them, giving WSR the home court advantage in a regional final.

Unfortunately, our string was broken as Waukee came out hot, and we came out flat, losing by 23. I was really disappointed after the game and thought for sure we would be dropped below W-SR and lose our advantage. Fortunately, we had beaten W-SR earlier in the year at their place, and the union kept us ahead of them. It was a huge relief, but we knew we were going to have to play well to make it to state again.

At the end of the season, I felt our team really came together and was totally "all in" with what we wanted to do. Coach Trask was a big part of that and helped us develop two "catch phrases" that got everyone energized and gave us a lot of laughs as well as a lot of calmness. Many of our bus trips and locker rooms were filled with "LET'S GO" and "SLAY" depending on the situation. If you have ever been part of a team, you understand **the importance of having things that pull the team together as well as keeping the fun factor involved.** Those phrases did that.

Our first opponent was Decorah, a team we had seen play in person in a game where their point guard had over 30 points and showed how good they were. We had other tape, and I felt our players were taking them lightly because of whom they had played during the season. Fortunately, we jumped on them early and had a 20-point lead in the first half. However, in the third quarter, we hit a funk and were just 3 of 15 from the field, allowing Decorah to cut the lead to two. We slowed the game down in the fourth quarter and hit 11 of 13 free throws to win by 12. Not the prettiest of wins, but they are all pretty in the postseason! W-SR won their game so we were set to host them in our gym in the regional final.

I think the players were pretty confident going in as one of W-SR's best players was out with an injury, and we found out right before the game that another player of theirs would miss the game as well. I did remind the players that our situation was the opposite of last year. We were hosting a team we had beaten earlier in the year. We did not want the outcome to be reversed like the previous year. The crowd was huge but almost immediately, we found out that this was going to be a fight. Waverly led the whole first half, and their crowd was incredibly into the game. You could tell our nerves were high, and we were feeling the pressure to win, especially at home.

The back and forth continued into the fourth quarter with no team having more than a 4-point lead the entire game. We were able to get a small lead with a little over two minutes left and had decided to shoot nothing but layups, something we had done very successfully over the years. Our best player drove to the basket, knocked one of their players over, and they called her for a charge and her fifth foul. This was obviously a huge loss, but we felt good as we still had the lead. Unfortunately, WSR came down the floor and scored immediately to take the lead. We had several shots to take the lead with under a minute left and missed them all so we had to foul WSR who proceeded to make both to take a three-point lead with under 30 seconds to go. We advanced the ball to half-court and called time out.

Call it a stroke of luck, divine intervention, good coaching, or whatever, but the day before, for some reason, I had decided to practice a play that we had used in previous years but had not practiced it all year. It was designed to get us a 3-point shot or at least an open drive from the side out-of-bounds. When we went to the huddle, we told the team we were running "Square" and put our freshmen in the position of the 3-point shooter we were trying to get open. The play was right in front of our bench. We threw the ball in, and our freshmen set a screen, came off a screen, and popped out to the wing with room to shoot. She calmly caught the ball and knocked down the shot! It was definitely pandemonium in the gym! Watching the game tape later from two different angles was amazing to watch our crowd go from despair to euphoria in such a short period of time!

WSR came down, called time out, and had a shot to win that was off the mark, sending us to overtime. We knew it was a tough task without our best player, but my words to the team were simple. "They had their chance to beat us; we aren't losing now!" Overtime was as exciting as the rest of the game with a couple back and forth baskets and some excellent defensive plays by both teams. WSR took the lead with just over a minute left in OT when one of our senior posts, an excellent shooter but definitely one of the quietest people on the team, found herself open at the 3-point arc. Without hesitation, she took the shot. It was nothing but net, putting us up one with 26 seconds left!

WSR still had time to win and took a bunch of time off the clock before calling timeout with just a few seconds remaining. Another state berth was ours if we could hold on! They inbounded the ball, and we got a bit out of position on top so the ball got passed to the wing. The shot went up right before the horn and is right on line, however, it went off the rim, and we were off to state again with a 55-54 win!

One of our parents took a picture at the end of the game. I had my hands straight up in the air as the coaches were charging at me. What an amazing picture that showed the incredible emotion we all felt. Friends have commented that I appear to be reaching out to Dad in Heaven. It was definitely unintentional, but he may have been giving me a quick high five! Mom is adamant that Dad helped knock that last shot off the rim. I'm not so sure Dad has that much power! We certainly needed all the help we could get against a quality opponent in such a pressure situation. That game will certainly rank high in the best memories of my career. Before the season, we told the team we had a chance to host the regional final in our gym, and what an amazing experience that would be. How true that turned out to be!

After all of the regional games were played, we were ranked lowest of the eight teams that made it to state so we knew we would be seeded eighth and play the #1 ranked team in Western Dubuque. They were a formidable team with a Division I center along with being two-time returning state finalists. They had the top-ranked defense in 4A as well as a very tall front line. However, we relished the underdog role and knew we could go 3-0 just as easily as 0-1. Our mantra was to go 1-0 three times, the same thing we said after the Cedar Falls game and our record was 7-7. We would play our game and see what happened.

In the time leading up to state, I sensed a different vibe with the team than some of our other state teams. They were relaxed, focused, and very confident despite our #8 seed. We knew it wasn't going to be easy but as I told the team, we haven't done anything easily the whole year so why start now?

One of the coolest parts of our state trips was the school district allowing us to "tour" the elementary and middle schools and receive best wishes from the students and staff. Since our players attended those schools, it was a way for our players to say thanks as well as hopefully inspire the students to keep working hard so that they could achieve their dreams. The afternoon is always fulfilling but also wearing, so we decided to go to the schools on the Friday before state so everyone could get plenty of rest. As we made our way around, it was amazing to see all of the cards and posters students made for us as well as how excited students and staff were to see us. It was great recognition for the team and another example of how connected the school and town were to our program.

The game was scheduled for 6:45 on Tuesday, March 1st which worked great for us. We were used to playing in Des Moines on Tuesdays at that time so we drove down that afternoon after a pep rally and showed up to "Slay the Bobcats!" One of the cool things about making it to state like we have is seeing familiar faces at the Wells Fargo Arena when we get there. One of those memorable people is the person who greets us and gets us to our locker room. The first time we made it, she let us know her name was "Lois, but everyone calls me Lo Jo!" She proceeded to tell us a story about her ties to SE Polk, how long she had worked at the tournament, and her history with girls' basketball. Every year we hear the same basic stories, and every year Lo Jo has the same passion! Our team has learned to be patient and to enjoy the tradition of listening to Lo Jo. She is a great example of how many people it takes to put on a show like the state tournament and is also an example of **being passionate about your job and giving it your best, no matter what that job might be.** I'm sure some teams don't stop to listen to Lo Jo, but we will always be respectful and allow her to share her stories with us.

The game started interestingly enough as 10 seconds into the game, their star post player drove to the basket, clearly ran our player over, but she made the basket, and we got the foul. The free throw was good, and we were down 3-

0 after 10 seconds. I thought, here we go again. My history with officials wasn't the best as you remember! Fortunately, the officiating was excellent the rest of the tournament, and we had no reason to complain.

The game itself was back and forth the whole way. We led 14-8 after a quarter, but it was a one-point lead at halftime. The third quarter may have set basketball back a bit as they outscored us by a whopping 4-3 (it was great defense by both teams, right?) to tie the game after three quarters. The fourth quarter was back and forth as we trailed 33-32 with three minutes left when our senior post (who hit the game winning shot in the WSR game) drained a three from the right wing to put us up two. After a turnover, she got the same shot from the same spot with the same result! I distinctly remember a yell and a fist pump from her after the second shot, and probably the most emotion I had ever seen from her which sent our crowd into a frenzy! Like usual, we had one of the biggest crowds at the tournament and that continued throughout the week. A supportive crowd has so much positive impact on teams, and there is no doubt our crowd has been a big reason for the success we've had.

As we always do when we take the lead late in games, we ran our delay game (turtle) and forced them to foul us. It puts pressure on the players to make free throws, but we like our chances doing that, and it forces the other team to make shots while we are making "free" shots. Fortunately, the players were up to the challenge as we went 18-21 from the line and put the game away 47-39. We held them to 11 points under their season average and somehow out-rebounded their very tall team. The end of the game brought great joy and also relief as we had lost our first round game at state four out of the last five years (albeit to excellent big schools) and were thrilled to make the semifinals. Although the team was excited to make the semi-finals, their comments to the media after the game showed they wanted more.

Interestingly, all of the lower-seeded teams won their first round games so we were matched up with #5 Keokuk in the semifinals. Obviously, we knew nothing about them other than the game they played after us at state. They were not very tall but were very fast and pressed a lot so we knew the challenge was huge again. The semi-final was scheduled for Friday so we went home right after the Western Dubuque game so kids could sleep in their own beds, keep up with their classes, and keep some semblance of normalcy.

We decided to drive down to Des Moines on Thursday afternoon after having a normal practice in our gym. I had been in a discussion with our AD, Bob Kenny, about our plans after Friday's game. Would we stay overnight Friday night if we won or go home? Would we stay if we lost? In Bob's words, "I think you need to act like you are going to win it all. You need to stay down there Friday night and Saturday night so you can celebrate the championship!" Good advice! Bob also discussed with our custodians what our welcome home pep rally would look like on Sunday after we won. I did feel a bit uncomfortable talking to our Denny Luecht, our head custodian, about our celebration on Sunday considering we had two games left to play, but I was definitely buying into the win so plans were made for a Sunday celebration.

We hoped to get to the arena soon enough on Thursday to watch Cherokee, my former school, play in the state semi-finals. They won their first game, and Coach Trask thought it was a good omen that they won and that my first school, Newell-Fonda was also still playing at state as it was becoming the "Klaahsen Magical Mystery Tour" with my team and former teams winning. We watched Cherokee's first game on the computer before we left on Tuesday so we wanted them to win as well.

Unfortunately, we didn't get there soon enough so we went out to eat and watched the game on Coach Kirby's phone. It was halftime when we got there tied at 43. In one of the best games ever played at state, but Cherokee lost 102-91. Who says girls' basketball isn't exciting! I was very disappointed for Cherokee but very proud of the players and Coach Heath Hagberg who was a middle school coach when I was there and remains a good friend. It definitely got our kids pumped up for the semi-final game. The semi-final was scheduled for 10 a.m. Not a perfect time to play, but like we talked about frequently with teams, **it shouldn't matter what time you play, who or where you play, you should be ready to give it 100% and be at your best.** The team was focused and confident, and we were ready to go.

The motel we stayed at had amazing customer service. They greeted us warmly when we got there and had signs set up wishing us good luck! They went out of their way to make sure we had everything we needed and even gave us complete access to their conference room so we could have a team meeting place to go through a scouting report and watch tape if needed. In the future, if we ever make state again, we will stay there. The motel and staff had a very positive impact on our team and their families.

Keokuk was a very aggressive and quick team, so the game plan was to take advantage of that if possible while being aggressive ourselves. That started with the opening jump ball. We thought we could get the tip so we called for an "offensive tip" which is basically when we send kids flying down the court when the ball is thrown up and try to take advantage of getting the ball. When the tip went up, we got it, made one pass to our freshmen guard who laid it in. We were up 2-0 four seconds into the game!

On our first possession, we noticed they really overplayed our guards, so we called our best backdoor play to take advantage of it. It worked, and we got fouled. The third possession, one of our senior guards hit a three, so one minute into the game, we were up 6-0! I basically sat on the bench and watched those three possessions while our coaches and bench went crazy around me! I'm not sure what it was, but I was supremely confident about that game and our kids played with confidence as well. We led by nine after a quarter, by 12 at the half, and as much as 17 at one point.

Unfortunately, we had another bad third quarter and Keokuk cut the lead to five early in the fourth quarter. However, as in the first state game, we followed a tough stretch with some great basketball, closing the game on a 14-7 run, winning 57-45 to make it to the championship game for the first time ever! Once again, the kids were clutch under pressure, making 21 of 26 free throws including 15-17 in the second half. In the first two games, we were 39-47 at the free throw line for 83%, an almost unheard of number!

I get asked a lot how our kids stayed so calm with all of the pressure on them especially when teams came back on us in all of our state games. I just think being the eighth seed helped tremendously and as a staff, we stayed in the moment while always going back to the "go 1-0" mantra. We were going to make sure the team stayed positive, and we never focused on winning a championship but winning the next possession.

Geno Auriemma, the amazing University of Connecticut women's basketball coach has a great quote that we should all remember when under pressure situations, "Fear paralyzes you; the desire to win inspires you." He talks about embracing the moment and not being afraid to lose. It's hard to follow through with those words, but I thought our team did that throughout the tournament.

I stayed quite calm until the very end when we made a couple big plays to wrap up the game. The papers took some fun pictures of our coaches and the bench getting excited at the end of the game including one that made the front page of the Des Moines Register. I will never apologize for my passion and just feel incredibly blessed that I can have a job that gives me moments like that which can be shared with so many people I care about!

One of the advantages of playing the first game was that we could scout the second game and get an idea of what we would have to do to win. Fortunately, my trusty assistants went right to work watching game two while I took care of the media obligations. Pella and Marion were similar teams. They were not real tall (thankfully for us!) but young and very talented. The game was back and forth so we had to watch both teams closely. Eventually, Pella pulled it out so we went to work preparing for them.

Something that is always a concern when you play an opponent is how much do you scout, how much information do you give the team, should you just focus on yourself, etc? We have always prided ourselves on being well prepared, but throughout the tournament, we had spent much more time focusing on ourselves and taking one game at a time. Since the beginning of the season, we had not talked about winning state. We had focused on the next game, giving our best effort, and staying in the moment, one play at a time. As a coach, you worry about players getting caught up in all of the hoopla, especially with media and family talking about a possible state championship, what it would mean, etc. I felt good about our team going into the Pella game, and as I listened to our players talk to the media after the Keokuk game, all I heard was how focused they were and how they were taking it one possession at a time. Mission accomplished!

We decided to keep it low-key Friday night and Saturday before the game. The motel we stayed at was perfect for that, and we were across the street from a mall so the plan was to keep kids occupied while coaches watched tape and worked on a game plan. We set up a shoot around with Waukee's coach, Chris Guess, for Saturday morning, and headed over to take advantage of the practice time. As the team shot around, the coaches and I talked to Chris about his experiences as his team had won the 5A state championship the previous year.

He relayed that the night before his championship game, he was spending hours going over tape, thinking about strategy, and what he needed to do to beat Valley as he had lost to them earlier in the season. He was looking for the magic idea to win the game. Finally, his wife, who was his assistant, looked at him and to paraphrase, said, "Quit overthinking about it; let the kids play, have fun, and quit over-thinking it!" He decided right there to not change up what his team did but instead just play their game and see what happened. Waukee had played loose and relaxed and won the championship game by 14. I was excited to hear Chris' advice as that is what we had been doing during the entire tournament trail. Chris was kind enough to relay his message to our kids, and we left Waukee very confident about our chances and ready to go. The afternoon wait was LONG because we didn't play until 6:00, and we let the kids choose how they spent their time.

I had a note from my mom that we were going to have some special guests at the game. The Van Briesens were close neighbors of the folks, and their boys would stop frequently to see them. Mom always had the candy dish stocked and lemonade on hand, and the boys loved visiting the folks and making themselves at home. When Dad died, it was especially hard on the boys as I think they saw Mom and Dad as another set of grandparents and down to earth people they could relate to despite the age difference. Mom's note mentioned that the Van Briesens decided at the last minute to drive to the game and the middle son, Dalton, a junior in high school, had wanted Dad to be represented at the game and didn't want Mom to be alone. So, he decided to wear overalls to the game! What a touching tribute, and I felt like with Dad's presence at the game, how could we lose? Dalton ended up wearing overalls for one of his senior pictures, and I'm sure Dad was very proud of him for that!

When we loaded the bus, you could tell the team was nervous, but we did everything we could to keep the mood light. As we had used as our mantra during the tournament trail, the words "LET'S GO and SLAY" were said many times on the bus ride to the arena. No matter what, we were going to have fun and embrace the moment.

We got to Wells Fargo Arena at the start of the 3A championship game before us so we got to experience the "hoopla" associated with a game on TV and how the introductions would work. It was great to see Pocahontas Area playing in that game as we knew the coaches very well and the whole team was a class act. They had lost the state championship game the year before and were on a mission to win it all, which they did!

When we got to the Arena, one of the IGHSAU officials mentioned that at halftime of the 3A game, they wanted to meet with me and Jerod Garland, the coach at Pella, to go over how the game would go behind the scenes and what we needed to be aware of at the start. When we met, Jerod and I had a great chat. You could tell what a class act and what a great coach he was.

The people from the union let us know that we would be mic'd up during the game and to remember that, although there was a seven-second delay in what was broadcast, anything we said would be out on the Internet and would be impossible to get back. I joked that I was more worried about my assistants (mostly Coach Kirby!) than myself. OK, maybe I wasn't joking that much! It was a reminder of the large scale of this game and how many people would be watching. They also reminded us that halftime would be twice as long, about 20 minutes, and that the TV announcers would talk to the coach leading at halftime.

In the locker room before the game, we kept the talk short, reminding the players briefly about Pella, but we focused mostly on what we were going to do and to take things one possession at a time while staying in the moment. Fortunately, we had a large senior class who was incredibly focused, and with Pella having a young team, we thought our experience would come into play positively for us. I still can't explain it, but even through the championship game, I felt incredibly calm and almost felt in a peaceful "zone" with nothing else mattering except what was going out on the floor. People have told me maybe Dad was reaching down and helping me out a bit. There's no doubt I felt his presence throughout the tournament. I also realized our team needed that and knew that in previous years, I probably had not been as calm as my team needed. Teams usually follow their coach's attitude and example so I was hoping we would do the same this time.

Our team got off to another excellent start as one of our seniors hit a three 40 seconds into the game, and we took that momentum through the first half. Every time Pella got some momentum, we would make a play to halt the momentum. We also got some huge plays out of four of our bench players. Although they didn't score a lot, they had a number of rebounds and hustle plays which kept us going forward. Coach Garland mentioned after the game what a key our reserves were and what a great reminder about how everyone on a team has a role to play, and you never know when you are needed to step up and help out. Along those lines, our kids that didn't play had a huge part in the game whether it was supporting their teammates, echoing the coaches' play calls, or just keeping everyone involved in the game. Every player on the team contributed to the tournament games, especially the championship game.

We reached halftime up 27-20 so I had to do the halftime interview. One of the production people led me to the table where the announcers were so I thought I would be talking to them. I actually ended up talking to someone in an upstairs booth so I could not see my interviewer. It worked out fine, but it was awkward talking directly to a camera and not seeing the person you were interviewing with at the time.

Weeks later when I watched replays of the game, it was interesting to listen to and watch our huddles and how the announcers reacted to it. At one point, one of the announcers praised both Coach Garland and me on how positive we were with our teams and what good role models we were in working with young women. In the heat of a game, I'm not sure any coaches are focused specifically on that, but we do always need to remember that **no matter the circumstances in a game or practice, we are there to help young people grow, and we are giving them lessons they can take with them the rest of their lives. It shouldn't matter how big or how small the circumstances, we should always treat our players and others with respect and be a role model for all to follow.**

As I mentioned before, halftime was 20 minutes long so we gave the players some extra time before we went in. The coaches and I talked, and they mentioned possibly mixing up the defense we were playing to give Pella a different look to start the half and to continue our momentum. I must admit I was a bit leery of changing, but I trusted my assistants totally, and we made the change along with continuing to focus on one possession at a time.

Unfortunately, as was our pattern at state, we struggled in the third quarter, and Pella played with a lot of passion. Suddenly, we were behind with all of the momentum on Pella's side. At the end of the quarter, they had the ball with the lead but shot a bit early. We got the rebound, and our freshman drove the length of the court and hit an acrobatic layup at the quarter giving us the lead back. Looking back, it was a huge play, as they had all of the momentum and our kids were a bit down. You could tell we were energized between quarters, however, and ready for the rest of the game.

Pella took the lead again to start the fourth quarter after our freshman turned it over. However, the next possession, showing the unflappable nature she had all season, she turned around and hit a long three-pointer to give us a two-point lead, and one we would never relinquish. From that point on, our senior best player took over with a floater in the lane and a 25' bomb to suddenly put us up seven. We knew Pella would keep fighting, and they did, scoring immediately to cut it to five. However, despite some nervous moments, we hit enough free throws to take the advantage into the last minute. As we have always done with the lead, we pulled the ball out and made them foul us. Fortunately, we once again made enough free throws to hang on. Our best player hit her first 12 until finally missing with nine seconds left and the game in hand.

My only regret is that when she hit a free throw to put us up seven with nine seconds left, I did not sub our bench and give them a chance to experience a championship game. You never think the game is over but at that point, it would have taken a miracle for the other team to come back. It would have been a perfect way to honor a group that was such a big part of the championship, but I think they were OK without the moment. When the last second ticked off the clock, it was an almost surreal moment. The coaches all embraced, and the emotion was overwhelming! A few years back, we had watched a championship moment where a team's coaching staff showed no emotion and barely shook hands after winning it all. We promised we would never act that way when we won it, and we didn't here!

One of the coaches mentioned how proud Dad must be. It's hard to describe how much he was on my mind at that moment. It was joy in the win but sorrow that he wasn't there. However, I knew as our senior had said after he passed way that he would have the "best seat in the house when we win the championship!" How true that was!

Once we were given the championship trophy and the all-tournament team awards were given out (our senior was the captain of the team and her freshman sister also made the team), we had a brief TV interview and took a team picture before leaving the court. Before we left, I made a mad dash to the stands for a quick embrace with Margo, Mom, and some other friends and family. That was the first time that the true emotion of the moment hit me. Dad wasn't here to experience it, but everyone else was as emotional as they had ever been.

One of the greatest joys of winning state was having much of my family at each of the games to celebrate with us. Margo came with the team, her parents were at each game, and my mom and siblings along with other numerous relatives were there as well, despite being a long distance from Des Moines. The support the team and I received from all over the state through calls, texts, and emails, was overwhelming. I've tried to reach out to friends and colleagues in similar situations, and now they were doing that for me.

My nephew, Kory took a great video at the end of the Pella game of the clock running down and Mom's reaction with tears running down her face. I'm sure there were a few tears of sadness that Dad wasn't there, but many more tears of joy for us finally having the ultimate success. My reaction was pretty similar. My first thoughts after the game were of Dad and how proud he must be looking down!

State Championship Team; photo courtesy of Jim Kirby Photography

As you can imagine, the locker room was a scene of unimaginable joy! All of the hard work had paid off, and as we talked a bit, it began to sink in that we would not be together in the locker room as a team like that again. Once the coaches finished speaking, as she was want to do, our senior leader raised her hand and asked to speak. The first thing she said was how thankful she was to have the coaches and teammates she did and how important we all were to her. How perfectly said that was! Before we left the locker room, we reminded the team that although this was the last time we would be together, they now had another family for life. As coaches, we would always be there for them and were only a call or message away. Those are big words, but I have always meant it and have tried to follow through with that. Although I don't have children of my own, I feel blessed to have had hundreds of "kids" who have given so much to me over the years and are the reason I work so hard at what I do to make sure they have a great experience. The biggest joy I have in life is seeing these young people continue to grow and become great parents, workers, and leaders themselves. I feel overjoyed at having a chance to be a small part of that development.

After the game, we went back to the motel and had a pizza and pop party with the team and their families. It was nothing fancy, but we were surrounded by the people that mattered the most. We set up the championship trophy and flowers so that everyone could take pictures if they wanted. My family did the same. Again, it wasn't the same without Dad, but we all knew how proud he was of this momentous accomplishment. When our families left, the coaches and most of the players stayed up late into the morning and watched a rebroadcast of the game. It was surreal watching it again but also quite enjoyable knowing the outcome!

The next day, we headed back to Mason City for a welcome back that had been set up earlier in the week. We stopped at the south edge of town and met up with fire trucks and police who escorted us to the high school. As we got closer, we began to see people lined up on the streets that were honking their horns and waving at us as we drove by. By the time we got within about 10 blocks of school, there were people everywhere along the streets! As we drove up to the high school, I remember saying, "Holy crap, there are a lot of cars here!"

We had a great crowd in the gym to welcome us back which was not a surprise, considering the fantastic following we had received all season and throughout my time in Mason City. It was great to be able to acknowledge everyone who had helped make this season happen. I especially made a point to have anyone who had coached our team previously to stand and be recognized. My coaches and I were getting recognition for our players' success, but ultimately, without the help of youth, middle school, and skills coaches, none of this would have happened.

A funny thing happened during the welcome back. While I was speaking, suddenly the microphone cut out and no one could hear anything; in fact, the speakers above were making some odd sounds. After it happened a couple of times and finally came back on, I looked at the ceiling and said, "Dad, are you messing with us? I know you want to be part of this, but you should leave this alone!" It got a good laugh, but part of me thinks he was pulling a little prank like he loved to do!

After the state tournament, we had a terrific but emotional banquet in which we honored the great achievements of not only the team but also especially our seniors who had done so much for the program. It was hard to see that group leave as they were such great young people and had worked so hard for me. They were third graders when I first arrived in Mason City, and they had stayed the course over those nine years to reach the top. They are all on to bigger and better things, and I am incredibly proud of them and all of the players I have had over the years. As I reflected, I realized it was also the first time in 29 years of coaching that a varsity season had ended without a loss! **It shows how in sports, and in life, we are at times going to have more losses than we are wins. How we deal with adversity many times will determine how successful we are going forward.**

Once the banquet was over, life didn't really turn to normal, as I made a major change in my educational career. In the last few years, Iowa has offered Teacher Leadership opportunities for teachers to move out of the classroom and into positions designed to work with and essentially "coach" teachers while in the process helping students achieve at a higher level.

I won't lie that in the previous few years, I had followed the TLC movement closely as I thought I would be a good fit for those positions. Also the last few years of my teaching career were "challenging" in many ways. Student behavior had become an increasing problem, and I felt my patience had gotten less over time, making my time in the classroom less enjoyable and in some ways, less effective. I had also taught the same curriculum for a number of years, and I would say that maybe I had gotten stale in my social studies position.

It was a risk to apply for the TLC position as there were no guarantees that these positions would continue to be funded over time, and I would be leaving the security and stability of my classroom position. However, during my career, I think I've always had an innate sense of when it was time to move on to something else and to not be fearful of the negatives of what could happen and instead be optimistic of the possibilities. So, when TLC was approved in Mason City, I knew I was going to apply for an instructional coaching position. I had been a finalist for a data team position a few years back, and I was hopeful I would be more successful this time. I was called in for an interview, and I thought it went well. I was excited for the opportunity to give back to others so many things I had learned over the years as well as for the opportunity for new learning myself through the trainings we would have.

After a long wait, I received word that I would be one of eight instructional coaches hired by the district. I was thrilled and assumed I would be assigned to my middle school building. However, I received word that I had been assigned to our intermediate building instead. Although disappointed and quite surprised by the decision, I was excited to get started and began planning on how I could make an impact on the intermediate teachers and staff. The trainings for my new job along with basketball activities made for an exciting and busy summer of 2016.

I've always believed that we should all be **lifelong learners and constantly try to improve our skills.** It would have been easy to spend the rest of my years in education going through the motions in my regular classroom until I retired, but I knew there was more I could learn and more that I could offer people. So far it has been a great move that allows me to keep coaching basketball and still have an impact on student learning now through working with and learning from great teachers. My goal is to continue to learn and share that learning until I retire!

CHAPTER 23

LESSONS LEARNED FROM 29 YEARS IN EDUCATION

Learn From Everyone You Meet

It would make for a great story here to say how much winning state changed my life, made me a better teacher, person, or coach, but I don't feel that is the case. Sure, it has probably given me satisfaction and probably more confidence to have achieved at the highest level, but **no one should be judged on the number of championships they've won.** If my coaching career had ended without a state championship, I would still have rated my career as a success because of the impact I have been able to make on the young people, coaches, and parents I have worked with over the years. There are amazing teachers and coaches all over the place doing incredibly good work who don't win championships, don't get named teacher of the year, and don't get promotions. Those teachers and coaches are in it for the right reasons and don't do it for the pay or for the recognition. Just because you have a title doesn't mean you are a leader! Thank goodness that we have people like that in the world!

Life should never be about winning championships. It should be about the process of working hard every day, learning from the people around you, and getting better (not getting worse). It should be about the journey we have taken, the people we have impacted and that have impacted us along with the relationships we develop. Ultimately, that is going to make for a more meaningful life.

Sometimes in this era of social media, I worry about all of the focus on how successful everyone is. It gives a false sense to others that maybe their life isn't good enough and brings negativity to their lives that isn't necessary. **We will all ultimately be judged some day on what we have done with our lives and what our legacy was. At the end of the day, we won't be judged by the money we earned or the awards we received, but rather by how we lived our lives and how we treated others.**

Unfortunately, we are definitely in the "me" generation from social media to "everyone wins a prize," and even to our political leaders. We don't see as much emphasis on "we" and working together as we need to. Thinking of this reminds me how blessed I have been in my life and how much I have learned in 50 years of life. I think as I have gotten older, I have tried to do much more to give back to others and to help others. Interestingly, the more I have done this, the more personal and professional successes I have had. I don't think it's a coincidence. Here is my attempt to "give back" to my readers and what have I learned in my life's journey that I think will be helpful to others:

FAILURE ISN'T FOREVER; IT DOESN'T LAST; LEARN FROM IT AND MOVE ON

I have been fortunate to have had some great successes in my professional career, however, I have also had my share of failures. All I need to think back to is my first Cherokee volleyball team that didn't win a match until our last tournament, my first basketball team at Mason City that went 2-19, or my losing three state tournament games in heartbreaking fashion. If I look at my coaching career, I've won almost 300 games in basketball, over 200 volleyball matches, and over 100 baseball games. However, I've also lost about 35% of the times during those events.

If I relate that to my teaching career where testing has become a huge part of all teachers' educational world, I would be labeled as proficient. I feel the same way in the classroom. Just because a student isn't at 90% on a standardized test doesn't mean he or she is a failure. **If that person is giving his or her best effort and learning and improving every day, then we should be labeling that individual a success.**

I must admit that I did not deal well with losing in my younger days. I took it personally and felt I wasn't as good a person or a coach as I could be because of losing. I feel fortunate that a lot of that changed for me when I met Margo. She gave me a new perspective and has always helped me focus on the next day or the next experience.

When we fail, it gives us a chance to gain some perspective and remember exactly why the loss should be the worst experience of our lives. Obviously, getting older has also given me a different perspective as has losing loved ones and close friends. Really, in the grand scheme of things, how important is a loss in a sporting event? Has my world changed drastically for the worst if I lose to Valley or Waukee? Instead, can I use it to improve as a coach, teacher, or person, and model that behavior for others?

Failure also makes us appreciate success that much more. If we have always been the best at what we do, we probably haven't had to struggle at all to overcome defeat. Eventually, everyone struggles and how we come back from that will determine our future course of action. If we struggle and achieve success, we will know the hard road to get there and will work harder to stay there not wanting to repeat the struggle we just went through.

I don't want to go off on a tangent here, but this is something that bothers me about youth sports today. So many adults especially get so wound up about whether youth teams win or lose and whether their kid is better than another player. When that athlete fails, the blame falls either on the coach, the official, or on a teammate. It's like the world will end if that young person fails.

Sorry, adults. We all know kids are going to fail a lot in life. It's OK if they lose a youth game as long as we model proper behavior and help them learn from those losses. They may play well and yet the team loses, they may play poorly and win or lose, or they might not play at all and feel like they should have played. Most kids aren't going to be great at everything they do as adults, so we need to make a decision about how we are going respond and then model that behavior. In my view, **our attitude is always our choice.** I hope people think about this before every athletic event they watch and decide how they are going to help their young person during and after the event.

If your child isn't playing, or if you feel like the officials aren't giving you a fair shake, are you going to be the loud parent who is embarrassing to be around, the parent that is going to embarrass their child during the game, or the parent that supports all players on the team and is supportive of your child after the game? Honestly, in 29 years, I've never seen the first two be positives for the player or the adult. Please choose #3 as that is what is best for everyone! I will now climb off the soapbox, but thanks for listening!

The point is easy. **Everyone is going to be unsuccessful at some point. Learn from failure, ask for help if needed, and work harder to be better the next time you are in that situation. Be a role model for others on how to deal with adversity and make it an opportunity for learning.** As adults, we shouldn't try to live the lives of our children or students. We can model and guide, but at some point, **children need to learn some things for themselves as well as developing problem-solving skills that will last a lifetime.** I sometimes like to ask parents who are always meddling in their child's situations whether they plan to do that for the rest of their lives, as that is the only lesson being taught to the child at that point. Usually, parents can answer that for themselves.

GIVE YOUR BEST IN WHATEVER YOU DO

I will never claim to be the smartest, the most athletic, the most creative, or basically the most of anything in life. God has given me some abilities, but certainly there are many others who can do more than me. However, I would hope that one of my best abilities is giving my very best effort no matter what I am doing. Even if it is a task that isn't one of my favorites, I always give 100%. I think people realize that when I am involved with something, they will get my best.

I have learned that lesson over the years mostly from my parents. We never had the most money, the nicest clothes, the biggest house, or anything else. However, I knew my parents worked their hardest to make sure my siblings and I had everything we needed. They always helped others when needed. They were always the first to volunteer for church or community activities. My parents never expected financial assistance for that. It's just who they were. My siblings have those same traits as well.

I think Mom especially has lived by the motto, "Do what needs to be done." I can remember when I coached baseball at Newell-Fonda, and we ran a 4th of July tournament. We would usually be short of workers, and the AD would need me to find someone to take tickets. The folks would drive down, and Mom would always volunteer to help. I think part of it was always that she didn't want to let people down and wanted people to succeed. It didn't matter what the task was. She was willing to jump in and help. I think it has bothered me over the years to watch students and athletes with great skills and abilities waste those because of a lack of effort or a lack of caring about what they were doing. **Talent can certainly take you places but without effort, you will never accomplish what you could accomplish.**

Unfortunately, I sometimes see that in the education world as well. It really frustrates me, for example, to be in teacher meetings and while someone is presenting, seeing teacher friends on their phones, playing games, searching the net, reading the paper, or some other activity. If these same people saw students doing this during class, they would flip out. Why is it OK for adults to then turn around and exhibit the same behavior when they get "bored" or believe something doesn't apply to them?

One of my favorite sayings is **"If you are going to do something, do it right or don't do it at all." It's a total waste of time to be involved in something and not give your best effort.** It's why I don't get upset when kids decide to not continue playing a sport for me. I would rather have them be honest with me and give up something than to continue and give a half-hearted effort. That sends a terrible message to the rest of the team who is invested and can cause serious problems for everyone on a team. It doesn't matter how talented someone is. If they aren't going to give their best effort, then you don't want them as a part of your team!

I get very frustrated with people who don't give their best effort because they don't feel their job is that big a deal or that they aren't getting paid enough for what they do. What a waste of time that is for not only that person but for everyone they work with. I'm a firm believer that **EVERYONE'S job is important and that it is up to us to fulfill our requirements to the best of our abilities every day.** If we are just putting in time, we should be looking to do something else.

WHAT JOB YOU HAVE DOESN'T MATTER!

I'll be honest. I have been to numerous trainings and had some jobs where my heart really wasn't in it, and I wanted to be somewhere else. However, I have looked at those as opportunities for me to learn and grow and maybe make a connection to others who have more passion about something than I do. The same has been true in roles I've had that I'm not thrilled with. I've tried to keep a positive attitude with those and make it a great experience for those I am working with.

To me, it doesn't matter what job you have. **What is important is what you do with that job and how you impact others.** I have seen hundreds of examples of secretaries, custodians, bus drivers, and teachers' aides at schools who have had a profound impact on people despite getting paid less than others at the school. **Every job is important, and you can impact others no matter what you do!**

Ultimately, we all have a choice as to what job we have and what our attitude is about that job. I ask that **everyone bring PASSION whatever you are involved with! Being excited about what you do will make the job better for you and for everyone you are working with.** If you can't bring the passion every day, then please walk away from that position and look for something else. **We owe it to the people we work with and see on a daily basis to bring our best each and every day!**

CONTROL WHAT YOU CAN CONTROL

Be honest. How much time do you spend worrying about things that you have no control over? All of us have things that affect our lives that we have no say over. Even the President of the United States, the so-called "most powerful person in the world," has things that he has no control over. For coaches, many times it's about what our opponents are doing. For high school coaches, it may be a lack of talent or height with our teams. For example, in 29 years of coaching, I have had exactly one girls' player who measured over 6' tall. Since volleyball and basketball have been two of the main sports I've coached, it would be easy to fall into the "woe is me, we have no height" trap. Honestly, if I had a dollar for every time someone said they wished they had more height, I could retire a wealthy man!

My response is that I don't have any impact on that so I'm going to do the best I can with what we have. How is it going to make my situation and especially my team better to complain about what we don't have and others do have? If my players or students see me complaining about what we lack or what others have, they are automatically going to believe that behavior is OK for them to do down the road. **Personally, think how much stress is added to our lives**

when we worry about things that we can't change.

So, how do we overcome worrying about things we can't control? A good place to start is the "Serenity Prayer" that we have all heard so many times: "God, grant me the serenity to accept the things I cannot change, The courage to change the things I can, And the wisdom to know the difference."

How many times have we all reacted in a negative fashion to something we have no control over? Has it helped the situation? I'm betting the answer is no. I can think back to numerous times I have reacted poorly to an official's call in my career. Did it ever change one of those calls? I can't ever remember that happening. In fact, it undoubtedly made the situation worse. I think over the years, I have gotten better at controlling that emotion, but it is still very hard. **When we fail to control those emotions that come over us, they only continue to grow and make us many times lash out at others who aren't deserving of that anger.**

The next thing that happens when we don't respond well to things we can't control is others pick up on our emotion and now think it is OK for them to respond in the same fashion. As a coach, why shouldn't assistant coaches and players respond in a similar fashion to us when faced with those challenges? My best advice is to **think first as to whether your actions can truly change a situation and respond accordingly.** Think about all of the people that are watching your actions at that moment and whether your response is modeling appropriate behavior and representing your true character. **Try looking at the "why" behind an event, and maybe you will get some clarity that will give you a better way to respond.**

For example, when I see a missed call by an official, I try to find a time to ask them what they saw with the call. Many times, he/she will say, "Coach, they caught them on the elbow. That's what I saw," when calling a foul. How can I stay upset when I hear that? It's what they saw. I may have seen something different, but it's hard to argue when an official tells me exactly what they saw. Asking why gives clarity, even though we may still not agree. I realize now that I wasn't very good at this as a younger coach (and it's still a battle!), but I know I have improved and show much more respect toward officials now than I used to.

As a teacher, I have become frustrated many times by decisions administrators have made. Maybe it's when a student comes back to my class after numerous issues or not getting something that I asked an administrator for to help in my teaching situation. Ultimately, administrators make decisions that are best for their building or district, and although those decisions can be frustrating at times, it is certainly within their right to make them. As long as they can explain the why, we need to move on and accept the decision without complaint.

Today's social media world has taken people's reactions to things they can't control to another level. No matter what side of the political world you are on, we all have seen hundreds (thousands!) of examples of people who voice their dislike of an action someone takes despite the fact that 1) that person has the power/capacity to do it and 2) a negative response isn't going to change anything.

I totally get that we are in America and have a right to voice our opinion. However, it has become so negative and so disrespectful today that people aren't thinking through the situation before typing an opinion and hitting send, and no one is truly taking the time to listen to what others are saying. What happened to disagreeing without being disrespectful? **It all goes back to controlling what we can control.**

FIND WAYS TO IMPROVE EVERY DAY

It is my belief that most people are interested in improving their way of life, be it their job, their work with their family, their life as a person, etc. and are looking for ways to be the best they can be. I feel this is one of my best attributes as a person as I am always looking for ways to get better. In fact, when people ask me, "Curt, what do you know?" my response always is "Not nearly enough!"

I've felt it is **each person's duty to be responsible for his/her own growth as a person, as an employee, and with everything that each person does.** One of my favorite phrases to use in basketball is when we are working on shooting. After we have gone through the basics numerous times and players have had to practice the correct form over and over again, I will ask the question "Who is your own best coach?" Almost always, someone will raise her hand and say "Coach Klaahsen!" Now I am obviously excited to hear that as I want them to believe in what I say and realize how much I can help them. However, the answer I want to hear is that **YOU are your own best coach.**

Ultimately, we all have to be responsible for what we do on a daily basis. **How we act, what we say, and how we treat people is all a choice that we make. We should be learning from everyone around us and every experience that we have. We should be reaching out to others who have different experiences or different/better knowledge than we do in order to grow. However, what happens after that depends on us. If we have the attitude that we are good enough at what we do and do not need to work to improve, then not only are we hurting our own future endeavors but are also hurting those around us and those we work with.** It goes back to what I have said before. **In everything we do, we are either getting better or getting worse.**

So how do we improve? Certainly we can each read, research, observe, and use many other avenues to improve our lives on our own. Many times people assume that if they just put in the time to do something, they will get better. For example, a basketball player who spends two hours shooting is going to improve automatically. I disagree with that. If he/she is not using proper shooting form or is going through things half speed, the odds of the player improving are quite low.

It goes back to one of my favorite phrases to use with students/athletes. **"You are much better off by incorporating quality work over a quantity of work."** That doesn't mean that putting time in isn't important, because it is. However, if that time is not using proper techniques or someone is not focusing totally on what he/she should be doing, then time is wasted and quality improvement will not occur. **The goal should be to train with "purpose" and make your time meaningful and not a waste.**

A common theme of my time in the classroom, on the court, or in the field has been, **"If you are going to do something, do it right, or don't do it at all."** Think about how much of our time and the time of others is wasted when we don't fully commit to whatever we are doing. It all starts with having a goal and knowing exactly what you as an individual want to accomplish. Hopefully, that keeps us on task and using our time wisely.

Clearly, based on my 30 years of work in the education field and especially my recent career change, a great way to make improvements in life is to have a coach or a mentor to work with in any position. There is a lot of evidence out there that working with someone through coaching or working with others to build "collective efficacy" is a great way to grow your instruction. Instructional leaders like Jim Knight and Diane Sweeney have spoken eloquently of the effectiveness of coaching, and John Hattie has shown the effectiveness of teacher efficacy with regards to student learning. Jim Knight says, "Effective coaching makes it easier for teachers to learn and implement new ideas. Indeed, without follow-up such as coaching, most professional learning will have little effect" (blogs.edweek.org).

In order to accept "coaching" or assistance from others, we need to understand that **no one is perfect, and it's OK to admit that we need help once and awhile. It doesn't matter how old we are or how much experience we have because we ALL can find areas to improve.** For example, I work with young people who have amazing skills and talents with regards to technology. It would be crazy for me to not lean on and learn from the expertise those young people have.

To me, **it is especially VITAL for those of us who work with young people to be continuously finding ways to improve to make sure students** are getting the best possible learning experiences they can when they are with us. Sometimes it may not be changing what we do all the time but possibly ADAPTING our work to fit with the group we are working with or the expectations put upon us.

What better way to get better at a skill then to partner up with someone who is not evaluating you but is looking at the big picture, seeing things from a different viewpoint than you, and someone who asks questions and makes you think about your practice? In my first year of instructional coaching, some of the best work I did was with very experienced teachers who were willing to open up their classroom and work with me to build practices that would improve student learning. **If we take our egos out of it and decide that "I want to keep getting better," then working with others can only be a positive.**

The key to effective coaching then is to view working with someone else as a "partnership" and not a situation where one person is better than the other and has all of the wisdom to pass on. Deep discussion and questions about a topic or skill is great learning for BOTH participants! It is fair to say I have undoubtedly learned as much or more during my coaching sessions with other teachers as they have learned. The best coaching in my mind comes when you have willing participants and when it is non-evaluative. Go back to what your vision or goal is for your career. If it is personal improvement and wanting to be at your best for others, then you should look at every avenue, including coaching, to make yourself the best you can be!

CHAPTER 24

WHEN LIFE MEETS COACHING
Where Do We Go From Here?

One of the questions I get asked frequently, especially by younger teachers and coaches, is what advice would I have for my younger self if I could start my career over? That's a great question although for the most part, I think I have made good decisions along the way and wouldn't change a lot about what I've done. I have very few regrets!

One thing I would change would be to **begin with the end in mind** as Stephen Covey talks about in *Seven Habits of Highly Effective People*. When I started teaching, I was happy to have a job and didn't worry much about putting money away, advancing in my career, and gaining new skills. I waited until my 40's to get my master's degree which not only kept me at a lower income but also kept me back from becoming more of a leader at my schools and doing more to contribute to students. Don Jenkins at Atlantic was a master at seeing the big picture with his students/athletes and making sure everything he did was geared toward ultimate success and lifelong lessons.

Another piece of advice would be to **value the process more and all of the steps it takes to get to where you want to go.** Definitely early in my life and career, I focused too much on winning and being successful instead of enjoying the moments and each opportunity that I had. Interestingly, as a coach, once I changed that mindset, my teams began to win more. I know I was putting too much pressure on them because of how competitive I was and how badly I wanted to win. I think the same has been true in the classroom as I sometimes pushed too hard for students to succeed, and I became too frustrated when it didn't happen. No one did this better than Jody Maske at Newell-Fonda for having a fun factor and staying in the moment.

Spending more time valuing the process would have helped me add more value to others. It's easy to become egocentric when working with others and make it all about YOU when it should all be about the other person. When we become unselfish and not so much interested in what's in it for us, our work becomes better, the trust we get from others increases, and everyone's experience improves. Ultimately, 20 years after we work with someone, what are they going to remember about us and their experience with us? As teachers and coaches, it won't be about the curriculum or about wins or losses. It will be about how we impacted them as people. Leo Hupke at Cherokee is one of the best I have ever seen at helping wherever is needed and always making it about others more than himself while having a lifetime impact.

Another piece of advice would be that life is going to be full of ups and downs so **stay positive and persevere no matter what comes up.** It's easy to get down when dealing with adversity but ultimately we must rely on our faith and those around us to keep going and get through any situation. **Don't ever stop believing.** There has to be a bigger plan for each of our lives! No one has exemplified that more than my parents who had 63 years of marriage and dealt with cancer, heart issues, alcohol problems, financial difficulties, family situations, and many more. Yet, ultimately, they stuck together, stayed positive, and always made it about others. How lucky I have been to have the parents I did!

Finally, one of the best things I have done throughout my career but can still do better and would advise everyone to always work on is to **build positive relationships with everyone you are with in every situation.** Ultimately, our journey through life is going to be judged on how we have impacted others and what kinds of personal experiences we have had. My late friend Jennifer Hutchens from Mason City was the best I have ever met. It didn't matter if you were an adult or a student, she made you feel important and that you were the most important person in the world to her.

Mom is also a great role model on how to build those positive relationships. I think a big part of why she gets along great with everyone is because she is a great **listener and is also very empathetic with everyone she meets.** She truly understands what other people need because she isn't in it for herself; she is all about others. Mom then takes time to respond to others and act on what others need while always being there when someone needs her.

I think one of my strengths over time has been being a positive teacher, positive coach, positive leader, and most importantly, a positive person. I have always tried to be optimistic and look at the bright side of things while working with others to make life better for not only myself but also others around me. I hear often that as people get older, they tend to lose some of that. I vow to not let that happen and instead follow the model my mom has provided all of these years!

My work as an instructional coach, my years of learning from great people, as well as my desire to work more with adults even after my career in education is over has led me to start thinking about my legacy though as I have spent my entire career helping kids in the classroom, on the field, and on the court. On my birthday, I received over 100 messages of congratulations, many referred to me as "Coach." I am very proud to be called that!

I am also very proud of the work I have done with students and athletes in the last 30 years, and now I want to expand on that and give back to others in similar situations. I'm not planning to work in schools forever, and if you know me, I won't just sit around the house in retirement! I want to continue to give back and help people in a positive way, now and in the future. After much thought and work, I have started a new program called *When Life Meets Coaching.* Our goal is to recruit, prepare, and mentor coaches from beginning coaches to experienced coaches and from youth coaches to college coaches.

One of my favorite phrases you've heard in the book is that "You are either getting better or you are getting worse." There is no staying the same. **Every person should be trying to improve every day no matter what his/her circumstances are.** There is plenty of research that shows the #1 factor in student achievement is a qualified, skillful teacher. States like Iowa have teacher leadership programs rolling for all teachers and mentoring programs for teachers in their first years of teaching.

However, what is being done for new and experienced coaches? Very little that I know of for these individuals. Athletic directors, YMCA and Parks and Rec directors, youth leaders, etc. have very little time, money, and other resources to help their coaches out to the extent needed. Many youth coaches are parents with great intentions but with no formal training and no one to help them out when needed. Many coach as they were coached which definitely doesn't make it right!

The National Alliance for Sports reports that 70 percent of kids quit playing league sports by age 13 and never play them again! Numerous studies show the positives of kids participating in extracurricular activities, and we need them to stay out and have great experiences! I think we can all agree that making sure sports coaches are well-trained and have continuous opportunities to improve could help keep more kids actively involved through high school, which gives us healthier young people!

Here's what it comes down to with regards to why I am starting *When Life Meets Coaching*:

• I want coaches to have great athletic experiences.

• If coaches have great athletic experiences, more than likely kids will have great experiences.

• If kids have great athletic experiences, more than likely parents and families will have great experiences.

Therefore, I want everyone to have a great athletic experience and it starts with the coach!!

There are many other reasons that something needs to be done to help coaches continue to learn and improve:

1. Not enough is being done to recruit, prepare, and retain coaches along with giving them a means for professional advancement down the road. Too many young people have a fear of the problems associated with coaching and choose not to pursue it.

2. Sometimes the least prepared coaches are faced with coaching the most vulnerable young people.

3. Studies say that 30% of teachers quit within the first five years, and coaches would be similar. Most get out because of low salaries, poor conditions, the unbelievable time commitment, and issues with parents.

4. Schools are finding it harder to find and retain coaches which is a financial issue for them and a bigger issue for athletes and their parents looking for a quality experience.

5. Youth sports continue to be extremely popular in our country. Coaches will always be needed.

6. New teachers have well-defined mentoring programs, and coaches don't have anything. According to the National Center for Educational Statistics, teachers with a mentor their first year were twice as likely to be in the profession after five years than those who did not.

Clearly, there is a need for a program to help grow coaches at all levels. I hope *When Life Meets Coaching* is a vehicle for helping coaches (including myself!) grow so that athletic experiences can be enhanced for all. If sports coaches have a "growth mindset" and are willing to learn and grow each day, WLMC has the potential to be a game changer with regards to youth sports.

As this book has shown, I have been incredibly blessed with all of the amazing people who have been a part of my life and allowed me to be a part of some amazing things. Although this book is my story and about the people who have influenced my life, each one of us has those people who have made a difference for us.

If I had to sum up what this book is about and what I have learned over the years, it's that life is about **people and the relationships we have with them.** It's easy to get caught up in money, position, power, politics, and many other things. Ultimately though, as humans, we are all in this life together, and we can all learn from each other, no matter what our differences. Although today's world often sees too much argument and disagreement with each other, don't let anyone fool you. The world is full of great people, and our days are always brighter when we are working together and not apart from each other. Politicians, are you listening?

My challenge to you is to think about who have been the people who have most influenced your life. Why have they had that impact, and how did they do that? I challenge you to reach out to them if you can and say thanks for what they have done. Also, challenge yourself to be that example and role model for the people who encounter every day. Everyone has a story to tell. Be that person who is going to listen to those stories and impact lives in a positive way!

I am so thankful to all of the people I have mentioned in the book and countless hundreds of others that I did not name who have impacted me in a such a positive way. I have been fortunate to live in a great state like Iowa filled with people who care about others and go the extra mile to help out where needed. I promise to spend the rest of my years giving back and supporting others like they have done for me!

CPSIA information can be obtained
at www.ICGtesting.com
Printed in the USA
LVOW13s1744220218
567560LV00013B/1530/P